Return to Cold War

To Gloria for everything

Return to Cold War

Robert Legvold

polity

First published in 2016 by Polity Press
Reprinted 2016(twice), 2018

Polity Press
65 Bridge Street
Cambridge CB2 1UR, UK

Polity Press
350 Main Street
Malden, MA 02148, USA

ISBN-13: 978-1-5095-0188-5
ISBN-13: 978-1-5095-0189-2 (pb)

A catalogue record for this book is available from the British Library.

Names: Legvold, Robert, author.
Title: Return to Cold War / Robert Legvold.
Description: First edition. | Malden, MA : Polity, 2016. | Includes
   bibliographical references and index.
Identifiers: LCCN 2015035827| ISBN 9781509501885 (hardback) | ISBN 1509501886
   (hardcover) | ISBN 9781509501892 (paperback)
Subjects: LCSH: United States--Foreign relations--Russia (Federation) |
   Russia (Federation)--Foreign relations--United States. | United
   States--Foreign relations--1989- | Cold War. | Security,
   Interntional--21st century. | BISAC: POLITICAL SCIENCE / International
   Relations / General.
Classification: LCC E183.8.R9 L395 2016 | DDC 327.73047--dc23 LC record available at
   http://lccn.loc.gov/2015035827

Typeset in 10 on 16.5pt Utopia Std by Servis Filmsetting Ltd, Stockport, Cheshire
Printed and bound in the United States by LSC Communications

For further information on Polity, visit our website: politybooks.com

Contents

Acknowledgements

Usually those who bring a book to print get thanked last, but this book would not be in print were it not for Louise Knight, Polity Press senior acquisitions editor. Prompted by a piece of mine in *Foreign Affairs* on what I called the new Cold War, she got in touch and challenged me to justify myself at book length. She and her assistant Nekane Tanaka Galdos cheer their authors on in a way that makes working with Polity Press a pleasure. The rest of the team at the press is also remarkably efficient and effective – none more than Caroline Richmond, who copy-edited the manuscript. Other authors will know what it means to have an editor who with small, deft changes tightens a manuscript without altering the author's voice. Caroline has that skill down to an art. To the anonymous outside reader who came to the manuscript skeptical of its theme, but with an open mind and willing to be persuaded – at least partially – I am grateful for the advice, even that which I did not take.

Were I to thank all those in the United States, Europe, and Russia whose writings and conversation over the years, particularly the last two, have shaped my thinking the list would be very long. Because none – with one exception – has had a chance to look at and try to rescue the manuscript, I will spare them. They will know who they are from my many intrusions on their workday and the pleasant lunches and dinners we have had together. I am deeply grateful for the time they have given me, the insights they have shared, and the friends they are.

Introduction

Five years ago – even two years ago – I could never have imagined writing this book. Talk of a new US–Russian Cold War, already in the air, seemed to me wildly exaggerated. Sure, tensions existed, and the relationship had been up and down for years. The two countries were feuding over US plans to put a missile defense system in Europe, the war in Syria, and the refuge Russia had given Edward Snowden. Vladimir Putin had run much of his 2012 re-election campaign on a crude theme of anti-Americanism. And President Obama had grown so frustrated over Russia's lack of cooperation on a number of key issues that he called off the summit of the two leaders planned for September 2013.

But that the bottom would fall out, and the two countries would careen into a swirl of vituperation, hostility, and confrontation with no end in sight, caught me, and I think most observers, by surprise. True, one or two commentators had for some time insisted that a Putin-led Russia was from the beginning in a new Cold War with the West. But most observers thought that either misrepresented the problem in Russia–West relations or misunderstood the concept of cold war. Now, however, suddenly the relationship had crossed a threshold and entered an unexpected but qualitatively different phase. The useful ambiguity of previous years, when neither side was quite sure whether the other was friend or foe (but, left to hope, mostly friend) had vanished. As the angry recriminations of spokesmen on both sides made plain, they were now adversaries, convinced the other side meant to do as much harm to their country as the former's scheming would allow. Thoughts of cooperating on issues where failure to cooperate bordered on the insane, such as limiting the spread of nuclear weapons, banding together to deal with terrorism, and doing something about climate change, still echoed faintly on both sides. But anything approximating genuine cooperation on the hard issues of the day, such as coping with a Middle East in flames, ensuring that the development of the Arctic's vast oil and gas reserves remained peaceful, getting a handle on the rising perils in a world of multiple nuclear powers, encouraging mutual energy security in place of increased energy competition, and responding to the rise of China and other new powers, had died – at least until that awful Friday night in November in Paris.

Instead the United States, in something resembling an ersatz containment policy, declared its determination to isolate the Russian regime – driving it out of the G-8, cutting off key arms control negotiations, suspending cooperation in a wide range of working groups, mobilizing allies to do the same, and, with them, applying a broad range of sanctions against Russian political and business leaders as well as key banks and energy entities. Russia lashed out with a bitter denunciation of US foreign policy and declared its willingness to live without the West – characterized in any case as morally corrupt and in economic decline and political crisis. It would use the West's hostility to develop its own human and material resources and create a more self-sufficient country. It would fashion an alternative universe of partners and allies – first with its nearest neighbors in a Eurasian Economic Union and then with China and the other members of BRICS (Brazil, China, India, and South Africa). And it would not back down: having seized Crimea and fueled the war in eastern Ukraine, it meant to keep supplying the insurgents with more and better armament and doing little to bring about a stable Ukraine at peace.

Something fundamental had happened in US–Russian relations, and more broadly in Russia's relations with the West, but what? How was this new dark chapter to be understood, its significance assessed, and its likely course judged? As analysts groped for a label, the easy recourse – too easy, because few thought hard about its actual relevance – was cold war. It was shorthand for a relationship gone bad, but whether and how this really paralleled the original Cold War went unexplored. Like the word "war" itself, when employed as "the war on poverty," a "war on crime," or the "war against drugs," the phrase had no conceptual content.

Many others, however, objected to the very use of the term. Calling this latest, admittedly steep deterioration in relations a cold war seemed to them a misappropriation of history, and, worse, one sure to produce misguided policy. Nasty as the relationship had become, it scarcely matched a contest that dominated an entire international system for nearly a half century. This was a feud between a set of Euro-Atlantic states and Russia. China and much of the rest of the world would not be part of it. Nor did a diminished and troubled Russia come close to presenting the challenge to the United States and NATO that the Soviet Union had. Moreover, to the extent that the notion of cold war implied an old-fashioned geopolitical struggle, it made no sense in a world where the threats were stateless terrorism, the economic pathologies of globalization, the mounting sources of global disorder and the growing incapacity of global institutions to deal with them, climate change and the resource conflicts likely to follow, and the violent fire raging in the world of Islam. To make matters worse, if cold war became the mental framework of policymakers, the strategies they were likely to embrace would be overly aggressive and ill-suited to a challenge whose context, character, and stakes bore little resemblance to those in the earlier period.

At one level all of these objections were valid. Looked at from another angle, however, things were not so simple. Indeed, the tensions convulsing Russia's relations with the United States and its European allies were not recasting the character of international politics or, like a vortex, sucking in a widening circle of other states. Yet, treating this as a key contrast with the original Cold War overlooked how central a single relationship – that between the United States and the Soviet Union – had been to the larger setting. Had there been no US–Soviet rivalry, or had it ended much sooner, there would have been no cold war or, at least, not one that had the same intensity or lasted as long. In much the same way, a poisoned US–Russian relationship, even if no longer the core of the international system, still had the potential to warp and damage key dimensions of international politics – from the management of (or failure to manage) a multipolar nuclear world to the state of play in global energy; from the prospects of peace in the Eurasian heartland to how tension-filled the adjustment to the rise of China and other new major powers would be.

If that seemed a stretch, given the inferior weight of Russia when compared to the Soviet Union, the metric was wrong. Judged by gross but crude measures of power, such as GDP and defense spending, Russia, with a GDP one-eighth the size of that of the United States and defense spending roughly eleven times smaller, was hardly in the same league as it – or as China, for that matter. Add to this the crushing economic crisis seizing the country in 2015, and it was hard to believe that Russia remained a player on a global scale.

Change the measurement, however, and the picture looked quite different. As the world entered the second nuclear age – a new era of multiple nuclear actors in complex relationships – Russia, the other power with half of 92 percent of existing nuclear weapons, had only one peer, and, unless the two of them took the lead, nothing would be done to contain the dangers in a new and vastly more complicated "second nuclear era." If the measure was stability in and around the Eurasian landmass, again, few countries mattered more than Russia. To the extent that fossil fuels will remain the primary energy source for the global economy through the first half of the twenty-first century, Russia, with 45 percent of the world's gas reserves, 23 percent of its coal reserves, and 13 percent of its oil reserves, slightly less than half of which it exports – making it the world's largest energy supplier – obviously had a key role to play. For US policymakers struggling with the headline issues of the day – a Syrian civil war, the Islamic State, Iran's nuclear program, not to mention the Ukrainian crisis – the actions of no other country raised more concern than those of Russia. And, together with China, both veto-wielding members on the United Nations Security Council, Russia held one of the keys to whether the universal institution counted on to deal with the many cases of regional violence – past and future – would actually be able to perform.

So, a new Cold War between Russia, the United States, and its European partners – if that be the case – is, indeed, a serious matter. Calling the collapse in relations a new Cold War, therefore, has to be justified – particularly when US–Russia potential collaboration against the Islamic State would seem to belie it. That is one purpose of this small book. But the larger reason for the book and the label is to underscore the consequences of what is happening and to place current events in a broader perspective offering a better chance of exiting the exorbitantly costly path the two countries are now on. The failure to recognize the stakes – and, to an extent, the misrepresentation of the stakes – in the Ukrainian crisis simply extends the failure by both sides to weigh properly their stakes in the US–Russian relationship throughout the post-Cold War period. The book's third purpose is to suggest a course that, were leadership in both countries – and the stress is on both – to adopt it, has a chance of leading away from the current confrontation.

The thesis that underlies what the reader will encounter in the next four chapters is simple, although far from obvious, let alone instantly convincing for many. It consists of three linked propositions. First, the confrontation between the United States and Russia that began over the Ukrainian crisis in 2014 now has a depth and seriousness, making it a cold war, with all of its attendant consequences. Second, the two sides arrived at this point together, having failed over the quarter of a century since the collapse of the Soviet Union to overcome and often even to address the factors slowly, if fitfully, dragging the relationship down, until the Ukrainian crisis and ultimately Russian actions in that crisis sent the relationship spinning into this new unknown. Third, the only path out of the current impasse must be traveled together; change will not come through the triumph of one side and the capitulation of the other or through the good will and initiative of one side unreciprocated by the other.

Both elements of this thesis – i.e., that the deterioration in relations amounts to a cold war and that each side bears responsibility – will stir strong dissent. Whatever it is, many will argue, the deeply troubled US–Russian relationship is not a cold war, and a fair amount of energy will continue to go into listing the reasons why it is not. The other objection will be still more fundamental: holding both sides responsible for this outcome, many in both countries will insist, ignores the extent to which only one side bears responsibility. In the United States and the West they will stress that Putin's annexation of Crimea and surreptitious war in eastern Ukraine constitute the sole reason relations have gone over the edge. In Russia an equal number will contend with comparable passion that US interference in the Ukrainian events, abetted by NATO allies, against the background of a US policy increasingly contrary, even hostile, to Russian interests explains everything.

My frail hope is not to persuade those who hold one or both views that mine has more merit, but that they will engage the argument honestly, if only to strengthen their own. For others, Russians and Americans, with open minds, the hope would be that they come away from the book with a deeper appreciation of the stakes involved, ready to bring a broader perspective to the current crisis in relations and, whether accepting the specific policy prescriptions offered here, persuaded that the leadership of both countries needs to rethink the trajectory they are on and alter course.

The argument unfolds in four parts. Chapter 1 explores alternative ways of understanding what has happened in US-Russian relations and makes the case that, carefully considered, the notion of cold war best captures the scale and nature of the collapse. Fundamental differences between the original Cold War and the present situation are obvious and noted, but in five crucial respects what is happening today mirrors what happened then, particularly in the early phase of the original Cold War. These five parallels, I argue, bring then and now into the same universe. But, rather than leave it at that, I weigh with some care the various reasons said to disqualify the use of the concept. Next, in pursuit of the book's second purpose, I explore what I fear are the very large and underappreciated consequences of the new Cold War. These are introduced not to diminish the significance of the Ukrainian crisis, but to give a larger context to events and the stakes involved.

Chapter 2 reverses the perspective and considers ways to think about the original Cold War that shed light on the new Cold War. Its purpose is not to reassess the Cold War, to share what the new Cold War history teaches us about key Cold War events, or to engage the arguments among Cold War historians over the origins, end, and course of the Cold War. There are excellent books that do that (Leffler and Westad, 2010; Westad, 2013; Service, 2015; Wohlforth, 2003; Gaddis, 2005, 1997; Zubok and Pleshakov, 1996; Haslam, 2011; Kremenyuk, 2015). Rather, it is to exploit different angles used to understand the original Cold War with the aim of enlarging the framework available for assessing today's confrontation. In addition, there are important insights to be had in contemplating the principal "why" questions concerning the Cold War: why it occurred, why it took the shape that it did, why it lasted as long as it did, and why it ended when and as it did. These are also considered in chapter 2, because it is from them that comes a better sense of the Cold War's legacy and of the lessons contained in the history of those years.

Chapter 3 then turns to an explanation for how the new US–Russian Cold War has come about. The road, it argues, has been long and sinuous, marked by phases, with one phase containing the seeds deepening the damaged and distorted character of the next. The Ukrainian crisis is the dramatic exclamation point in the process, but it is not where the story begins. However, it is unique, because it represents a fundamental break in the sequence of phases. The phasing is over. The Ukrainian crisis has eliminated the prospect that any time soon the two countries will return to the good moments and the bad, to the ups and downs that characterized the previous stages in the US–Russian relationship. The intense hostility and tension of 2014–15 may well subside over the next two or three years, and the two countries may well get back to an active, if uneasy interaction. Unfortunately the alternative chance of the confrontation exploding into something much worse also exists, although the degree to which both by early fall 2015 seemed to be settling into a stalemate makes this less likely. But, even if what the future holds is an easing of the standoff, the two will still remain estranged, and each will continue to view the other as an adversary, no longer a potential partner in dealing with the major foreign policy challenges each country faces. And a good deal of each country's policy will focus on dealing with the other in those terms.

The thread, having wound from the definition of the problem and an assessment of its scale and significance through the perspectives and lessons derived from the original Cold War and an exploration of the path leading to the new one, ends in chapter 4 with thoughts about what would be necessary were the two countries determined to work their way out of the current impasse. That is, were they ready, as this book urges, to make the new Cold War as short and shallow as possible – thus, addressing the third purpose of this book. The course urged, as I recognize, is not where priorities are in either country. Nor is the mood among political leaders, politicians, the media, and publics in either likely to shift quickly in this direction.

History's kaleidoscope, however, will continue to turn – as it did dramatically on November 13, 2015. Predicting how the force of events – including the unnerving realization that the Islamic State is no longer a local but now a global threat – may reshape the political landscape within either one or both countries or between them remains an uncertain occupation. Surely the menace posed by the Islamic State argues for military cooperation between the United States and Russia and a closer alignment on ending the fighting in Syria. But getting from there to any real softening of the deep mistrust and animosity between the two is quite another matter. Only if leaders on both sides step back, focus on the costs of their new Cold War, and consciously set about shifting course will they begin to lead their two countries out of the morass described in the pages to follow.

1

Dueling Concepts

On March 18, 2014, Vladimir Putin strode through the high golden doors in St George's Hall to a chalk-white podium and, before nearly a thousand parliamentarians, regional officials, and other dignitaries, denounced the United States as no Russian or Soviet leader had in many decades: It and its allies, he said, "prefer not to be guided by international law in their practical policies, but by the rule of the gun" (Putin, 2014a). "They act as they please," believing that "they can decide the destinies of the world, that only they can ever be right," using force however they choose and manipulating or simply ignoring the United Nations and its Security Council when it stands in the way. He was not done. Amid his grandiose, emotion-filled justification for Russia's annexation of the Crimean peninsula, he continued to excoriate the United States. If you press "a spring to its limits," he said, "it will snap back hard." That was what the United States had done: plotting "color revolution" against Russia, "lying to us," making decisions "behind our back," such as with NATO enlargement and missile defense in Europe, and "trying to sweep us into a corner" for having an independent foreign policy. It was, he concluded in a soaring, but historically dubious charge, still pursuing the "infamous containment policy" that the West had directed against Russia since the eighteenth century.

Two weeks before, with Russia deeply implicated in the Crimean events, President Obama had accused the Russians not only of "violating" Ukraine's sovereignty and territorial integrity but of "steal-ing the assets of the Ukrainian people," as he announced travel bans on an unspecified number of Russians and Ukrainians said to be responsible for the aggression (Obama, 2014). This was soon followed by the first wave of sanctions against individuals and a bank thought to be close to Putin and his inner circle. The administration also worked hard to bring along its EU allies, knowing that US sanctions would not have much impact if not matched by countries whose trade with Russia was fifteen times larger than that of the United States. Eventually this first wave would be followed in July and September by two more ever widening waves of sanctions, freezing the assets and denying visas to dozens of Putin's closest confidants, closing credit markets to all of Russia's major banks other than for very short-term loans, and sharply curtailing US and European business with four more key sectors of the Russian economy: defense and high technology, energy, engineering, and metals and mining.

The economic punishment went hand in hand with a vigorous effort to isolate Putin's government, banishing it from the G-8 in March, shutting down negotiations over Russia's entry into the Organization of Economic Cooperation and Development (OECD), the club of indus-trialized market economies, suspending bilateral trade and investment talks, ending various initiatives in the area of military cooperation as well as negotiations on missile defense, and calling a halt to most of the twenty working groups under the US–Russia Bilateral Presidential Commission. The latter had been the background warp and woof of the Obama administration's effort to "reset" US–Russian relations – collaborations on everything from counter-terrorism to legal and military reform, from dealing with civil emergencies to cooperation on energy, the environment, and health.

Never, even during the original Cold War, had the United States and its European allies attempted to blacklist and punish as many senior Russian figures or target such a wide range of economic entities. Compared with Putin's visit to President Bush's Crawford ranch in November 2001, two months after the attack on New York's trade towers, when the two men shared a barbecue dinner, practiced dancing the Cotton-Eyed Joe, showed up at the local high school, and traded jokes over exercising in the Texas heat or Siberian cold, by any measure the relationship had badly deteriorated (Sanger, 2001).

Not, however, for the first time. Since the middle of the 1990s US–Russian ties had seesawed between relative comity and rising tensions, plunging to an icy low after Russia's war with Georgia in 2008. On the heels of that war, the Obama administration's effort to mend relations and move forward was the fourth attempt to put the relationship on a more durable and productive basis. Three times before the attempt had failed: first, with Moscow's sour reaction to NATO enlargement in 1997, then after the 1999 Kosovo War, and, again, from the Iraq War in 2003 to the Georgian War in 2008. So, the natural question was whether this simply represented the latest failure, and the real task was to explain why the two countries could not break this boom and bust cycle, why periods of raised hopes and accomplishment gained no lasting traction.

The alternative possibility was that the plummet this time was qualitatively different. Propelled by the Ukrainian crisis, the two sides had sailed over the cliff, and there would be no climbing back to sturdier ground allowing a fifth run at cooperation – at least, not any time soon. If so, the task changed. Policymakers and publics on both sides needed a framework allowing them to comprehend the depth, essence, and, most important, consequences of the confrontation their two countries were now in. What way of thinking would make sense of these events or provide enough perspective to allow sound guidance for future US and Russian foreign policy?

Not surprisingly the answer did not come easy. More surprising, however, the answers that did come stirred not merely disagreement but passion. In no instance was this truer than when the notion of cold war entered the analytical competition. Given the speed and scale of the collapse in Russia's relations with the United States and Europe, the natural instinct was to reach for a familiar label, not least because, over the years, cold war had become the handy way to characterize any relationship – personal, corporate, or national – that had grown bitter but stopped short of violence. Others, however, paused, convinced that this reflexive and relatively unthinking comparison missed the mark and did potential harm.

Some balked because they did not want to believe that relations, though severely damaged, had sunk to this point, and still hoped the worst could be avoided (Voigt, 2014). Others thought the comparison flawed in the extreme. As Oxford's Alex Pravda argued, the relationship does "not revolve around a global nuclear arms contest" as in the original Cold War, nor are the sides locked in "a universal and existential struggle between social systems" (Pravda, 2014). Worse, he said, echoing the thoughts of many, the "new Cold War narrative" strengthens those in Europe and the United States urging the isolation of Russia and calling for a renewed policy of containment, a course likely to harden Russian policy and lead to greater aggression on Russia's part. Thomas Graham, George W. Bush's former senior Russian advisor, agreed, and added that it was arch-folly to think that the United States could isolate or contain a country that had one of the world's ten largest economies, was the world's largest exporter of hydrocarbons, and could count for relief on the BRICS, none of whom had any intention of isolating or containing Russia.

The "new Cold War narrative" that they attacked was, in fact, not all that new. A few observers had been arguing for years that the West was, again, in a Cold War with Russia, only Western leaders did not know it. Edward Lucas, *The Economist*'s senior writer on Russia, in his book *The New Cold War*, warned of a Russia not only under a despotic hand, hostile to democratic values and institutions, but also a menace to its neighbors, whose independence it meant to destroy, and no less to Europe and the United States, since the whole thrust of its policy aimed to do "harm" to the West, to "frustrate us, and weaken us" (Lucas, 2007). Stop the wishful thinking, he pleaded, and focus on "winning" this "new Cold War." Blunt the money and energy resources Russia was using to advance its malign agenda by denying the Russians capital markets; pay the unavoidable price of freeing Europe from dependence on Russian oil and gas; kick the country out of organizations where it does not belong, such as the G-8; and go to battle, trumpeting the virtue of Western democratic values over the evil of those animating Putin's Russia. (Seven years later, it might be noted, US and European leaders who in 2014 dismissed the notion that the collapse in relations represented a new Cold War were doing pretty much everything Lucas called for to "win" a "new Cold War.")

Lucas was hardly alone. Another British journalist, Mark MacKinnon, also published a book with the same title and largely the same theme (MacKinnon, 2007). In the United States, early in Putin's first presidential term, Senator John McCain had been sounding the alarm over Russia's bullying of neighbors, manipulation of energy supplies, intention to reconstitute the empire of Imperial Russia, and descent into tyranny with its security forces run amok. In 2005 McCain, joined by Senator Joseph Lieberman, had introduced a Senate resolution demanding that Russia be suspended from the G-8. Then, and in the years that followed, McCain and Lieberman had more than a few allies in the Congress and on the editorial pages of US newspapers.

The vindication that Lucas felt as the Ukrainian crisis exploded in 2014 (he quickly reissued his book and boasted, "I told you so") did not persuade the doubters. For the earlier period, even if one shared his view of Russia's leadership and its malevolent aims, it would be hard to argue that a cold war was underway, if, as he maintained, Western leaders failed to realize it. A war does not exist until both sides fight it. By 2014 both sides were fighting it, but by then a far broader array of commentators had latched on to the cold war metaphor. It was the speed with which the label gained popularity that stirred a number of analysts to take a hard look at the collapse of relations, and to say, no.

Dmitri Trenin, one of the most serious of these analysts, did not come casually to this conclusion. He was, in fact, among the first to describe the dramatic rupture in relations as the beginning of "Cold War II" (Trenin, 2014b). After deeper thought, however, he decided that cold war was the wrong way to think about the transformation. "Today's situation," he now wrote, lacks the ideological focus of the conflict "between communism and liberal democracy" (Trenin, 2014a). While it has "a traditional military dimension," this is "as yet" not dominant. It has "global implications" but is "not central to the global system." And, most importantly, "unlike the Cold War," it is "not the organizing principle of either world politics or even the foreign policies of the conflict's main contestants, particularly that of the United States." Better, he concluded, to see the confrontation as a renewal of great power rivalry, and, if a historical parallel was sought, it should be the nineteenth-century Great Game between the Russian and British empires, the struggle over control of the gateway to the Indian subcontinent, not the post-World War II Cold War.

Trenin's reconsidered view of the tailspin US–Russian relations were now in scarcely made it milder or safer than a cold war. On the contrary, as he wrote by fall 2014, "In contrast to the Cold War," the new rivalry "lacks agreed, if unwritten, rules," suffers "a gross asymmetry in power," and is "utterly devoid of mutual respect" (Trenin, 2014c). Given "a near-universal lack of strategic thinking," he warned, "it is thus more prone than the US–Soviet conflict to lead to a collision in the style of 1914. The Cold War, after all, stayed largely cold. There is no such certainty about the present situation."

Trenin's phrasing – a return to great power rivalry – flowed into a much broader and steamier debate. The drama over the exploding acrimony in US–Russian relations brought into the open a long-brewing argument over the very nature of the world facing the United States and its allies. The stakes were high. The issue was not merely over which academic camp's theory performed better. Deep in the entrails of the argument was whether US and European leaders did or did not understand the world in which they were operating and, therefore, whether they had botched two decades of foreign policy or, on the contrary, had set the right course, and only needed to adjust their sails modestly. Buried in the debate were very different notions of the challenge posed by Russia.

One side, best represented by Walter Russell Mead (2014) and Stephan Walt (2014), insisted that "geopolitics were back" – indeed, that they had never left. With the disappearance of the Soviet Union, the US leadership and foreign policy elite had embraced the gauzy illusion that crude power politics had also died. In the future, relations among nations would be softened and redirected, as Walt described their enticing vision, into "an increasingly democratic, globalized, market-driven, institutionalized, and allegedly benevolent world order." In scholarly circles this was known as a "liberal international order," but those who bought into it, Mead contended, had "fundamentally misread what the collapse of the Soviet Union meant." It may have represented the "ideological triumph of liberal capitalist democracy over communism," but certainly "not the obsolescence of hard power." The United States and its partners, the designers and beneficiaries of the system, had persuaded themselves that the rough and tumble political contests of the past made no sense in a world whose threats were climate change, failing states, religious and ethnic extremism and its scurvy offspring terrorism, along with a variety of ills spawned by globalization. But others, such as Russia, China, and Iran, did not agree, and, having nursed their grievances, when in a position to act, did so.

Viewed through this lens, the collapse of US–Russian relations and Russia's role in it presented no puzzle. The United States and its European allies, charmed by the notion that the age of *realpolitik* had passed, assumed that extending the institutions underpinning Western Europe's democratic peace to the Soviet Union's former empire was both constructive and in tune with the times. Russia disagreed, and it ended in the Ukrainian crisis. Starkly put – and no one put it more starkly than John Mearsheimer in a brash *Foreign Affairs* article in fall 2014 – the crisis was largely the "West's fault" (Mearsheimer, 2014). Major powers do not respond graciously to hostile alliances pushing up to their borders. The United States and its NATO partners should have understood that, by meddling in Ukraine – rallying to political forces hostile to Russia and set on NATO membership, a prospect Washington and Brussels refused to rule out – they were guaranteeing a predictably aggressive Russian response. It was, he wrote, simply "Geopolitics 101: great powers are always sensitive to potential threats near their home territory."

Russia's harsh moves to defend a vital strategic interest, Mearsheimer argued, scarcely meant that it was bent on grabbing all of Ukraine or the territory of other neighbors. If the West acted on this false assumption, it would make much worse a situation that its blundering had already made bad enough.

Mead, who shares Mearsheimer's hard-nosed view of power politics, took the notion of geopolitics to its logical extreme or, more accurately, back to its origins, and it led him to an entirely different assessment of the challenge posed by Russia. In the early twentieth century, Halford MacKinder, a British geographer, advanced the idea that whoever controlled the core of the European and Asian landmasses – what today is usually referred to as Eurasia – would rule the world. Geography met politics, and the field of geopolitics was born. In its original form it is not much referred to these days, but Mead seems to have it in mind when he identifies Russia, China, and Iran as three countries determined to prove liberal internationalists wrong – that is, determined to rewrite the rules governing what happens in their backyard. Their backyard is Eurasia, and all three, Mead contends, are hard at work redoing the expectations, territorial arrangements, and military understandings that once prevailed in this vital region. In short, according to Mead, Russia is not merely once again a normal power, playing normal power politics, but a revisionist power, eager to redesign who does what, when, and how in the approaches to Russia's borders.

Those on the other side of the argument think that Mead, Walt, and their allies mistake surface foam for the currents below. John Ikenberry, one of the most articulate and unbowed defenders of the opposing view, argues that the environment US leaders have crafted over the seventy years since World War II – a "far-flung system of multilateral institutions, alliances, trade agreements, and political partnerships" – still reigns (Ikenberry, 2014). Not only, he insists, are Russia, China, and Iran incapable of displacing the United States as the dominant force behind this order, they do not pretend to have an alternative model in mind. They lack the many elements that make up the power of the United States, as well as its geographical advantage and its far-flung network of alliances, and, in any case, they have no inkling of a better scheme by which to organize the world outside. What is more, they are, in fact, deeply enmeshed in the existing system, participating in its key institutions, using its rules to "advance their own interests," and benefiting from its openness to build their economies and draw on the dynamism of a global economy.

They may, indeed, resent US preeminence and wish to see it cut back. They may insist that their own voice be enlarged and that their national interests, even if disruptive, be recognized. But at the end of the day they are about "gaining voice within the existing order and manipulating it to suit their needs," not replacing it. Russia (and China), therefore, should be seen "not [as] full-scale revisionist powers but [as] part-time spoilers." Viewed properly, "worrisome" though Putin's theft of Crimea may be, Ikenberry says, it reflects "Russia's geopolitical vulnerability, not its strength." Putin may be "winning some small battles," but "he is losing the war," as the circle of democratic states and NATO allies draws closer to his borders. In a final wave of his hand, he writes: "Russia is not on the rise; to the contrary, it is experiencing one of the greatest geopolitical contractions of any major power in the modern era."

Cold War to the Rescue

Fundamental as this argument is, it sheds little light on the ravaged state of Russia's relations with the West – on the scale of the collapse, its likely course, and major consequences. Arguing over the nature

of the international system and the change it is or is not undergo-
ing may offer some broad insight into the context within which the
confrontation is unfolding, but it explains little of the dynamic within
this confrontation. Disputing whether Russia should be seen as a
rogue state determined to wreck key aspects of the international order
because crude geopolitics are again ascendant, or, on the contrary,
whether it is only a disgruntled spoiler condemned to rage against
arrangements it dislikes but doomed to fail in the long run because it is
out of step with the basic logic of current international relations, may
set a framework for labeling the challenge Russia poses. But it does not
create a basis for determining whether it is one or the other. Contesting
the offensive or defensive nature of the impulses driving Russian
behavior may help clarify a starting point in formulating a Western
response. But it begs the question of what kind of mess the two sides
are in and what it is likely to mean for the foreign policies of both, not
to mention its impact on the world beyond.[1]

Something else is needed: some other mode of thought or concept
that does justice to the turn US–Russian relations have taken; something that gets inside the train wreck and explores the damage done,
where the two parties are left and where they may go. At a more basic
analytical level, the need is for something that captures the effects of
rivalry between states rather than the large but loose ways that the
physiognomy of different international systems affects states. Rivalry,
indeed, is a place to start, but there is more than one way to think about
rivalry. One has already been mentioned: the nineteenth-century
rivalry between the Russian and British empires known as the Great
Game. From 1813, and the treaty ending Russia's war with Persia,
until 1907, when Russia and Great Britain decided that addressing
a rising German threat mattered more than the contest they had
waged over Afghanistan and its Central Asian hinterland, the two

dueled continually as Russia penetrated ever deeper into Central Asia, colonizing the khanates of Bukhara, Kokand, and Khiva, pressing on Afghanistan, and, in the fear-filled eyes of the British, menacing India, the "jewel" of the British Empire.

Maybe that is a way to understand the battle now underway between Russia, the United States, and the Europeans over the fate of the new "lands in between" (Belarus, Ukraine, and Moldova), with Ukraine as the strategic prize.[2] And maybe when, as in 1907, a greater threat (China? The Islamic State?) emerges, it will end in a new Russo-US collaboration. But the Great Game, while a friction-ridden clash over the space where two empires met, was only that. Long and fractious as the maneuvering was, it was over a fragment of geography, and not the most vital one at that. The Balkans held that honor in the nine-teenth-century Europe-centered international system. Nor did the Great Game subsume the whole of the Russian–British relationship. British and Russian rivalry in Central Asia and Afghanistan constituted an aspect of their relationship, not its essence.

Another concept of interstate rivalry, with a pedigree among aca-demic theorists, focuses on conflict-prone bilateral relationships that over time approach the threshold of war and sometimes cross it, not once but many times. Enduring rivalry, as this genre is called, does deal with elaborate, intense, long-term antagonism between two states. The central preoccupation of most who find the concept useful, however, is with war or the threat to go to war, not with the causes, nature, and evolution of the rivalry itself.[3] The concept originated when scholars studying a large database on the wars fought in the nineteenth and twentieth centuries noticed that many of them were between states mired in generally hostile relationships that had endured or would endure for years. The cases involved duos such as France and Prussia for much of the nineteenth century, Great Britain and Germany in the decades leading to World War I, and Israel and the Arab states after World War II. What in these particular relationships, they asked, disposed these pairings to settle matters through war? When do they fight? What about the balance of power between them, the range and history of their disputes, one or the other's level of dissatisfaction with the status quo, and/or the incompatibility of their political systems explains their willingness to cross the threshold and go to war? All of these are interesting and important questions, particularly when the objective is to refine general theories of war, but they are not terribly helpful in comprehending either what has happened in US–Russian relations, and why, or the precise character of the new rivalry and its likely effect on critical international problems.

Perhaps a third way of thinking about rivalry can do better. One of the notable qualities of international politics since the end of the Cold War has been the absence of strategic rivalry among the major powers. Strategic rivalry among major powers exists when one or more great powers see one or more other major powers as the primary national security threat, focus their defense effort on them, and form alliances against them. Strategic rivalry among major powers has been at the very heart of the international system, whatever its configuration, since the Peace of Westphalia in the seventeenth century. Its absence over the last quarter century represents a truly exceptional circumstance. Call it "the blessing."

Governments and publics have been so focused on the threat of terrorism, the chaos in the Middle East, and economic crises at home that the blessing has been scarcely noticed. Indeed, in many quarters the comforting impression has grown that the blessing is permanent – that, given deeply entwined economies, the nature of a globalized world, and the obvious folly of war between major players, the kind of rivalry that marked great power relations in the past no longer applies.

Conflicts of interest there will be. So too differences over the rules of play and tensions generated by conflicting approaches to specific problems, left-over territorial disputes, and injured pride. But the descent back to a time when major powers, such as the United States, China, Russia, Japan, and India, could, again, lock themselves in mortal strategic competition seems unlikely.

The trouble is that traces of the unlikely are already present. They exist in the uneasy balance between the interdependence the United States and China know they have and their growing fear that the other's military programs and long-term aims will eventually turn into an overarching threat. They reside in the steps India, Japan, and Australia are taking alone and together to guard against a menacing turn in the rise of China. They surely are now evident in the bitterness and hostile maneuvering that envelop the United States' relations with Russia.

In none of these cases, however, can it be said that a full-blown strategic rivalry has arrived. Even the angry US–Russian confrontation falls short. Neither country has yet officially identified the other as the first among the security threats facing it, although by summer 2015 senior US defense officials, including the new chairman of the Joint Chiefs, had begun characterizing Russia as such. Neither has reoriented defense programs that, in both cases, are midway through ongoing reform to make the military threat posed by the other the primary concern – although as 2015 unfolded both began adjusting military doctrines, defense budgets, military exercises, and defense planning in ways that moved in this direction. And neither has sought to fashion alliances aimed at the other. The United States has pressed its NATO allies to join its efforts to isolate and pressure the Russian regime over the Ukrainian crisis, but it has not attempted to draw others into a network of anti-Russian alignments. And Russia, as it goes about building a union with willing neighbors and promoting tighter relations among the BRICS states, acts with no illusion that either enterprise could be turned into an anti-American front.

The original Cold War between the United States and the Soviet Union did satisfy handsomely the criteria of a strategic rivalry. Each saw the other as the main threat. Each wielded massive conventional forces and amassed vast arsenals of nuclear weapons specifically designed for the other. And each labored hard to mobilize and, harder yet, to maintain alliances directed against the other. The United States fashioned a necklace of alliances around the Soviet Union, starting with NATO and extending through the Baghdad Pact and the Southeast Asian Treaty Organization to the US–Japan Security Treaty. The Soviet Union, having overrun Eastern Europe, turned it into the Warsaw Treaty Organization and, until the Sino-Soviet conflict erupted a decade later, embraced as anti-Western allies the communist victors in the 1949 Chinese revolution.

If the traces of strategic rivalry in the new US–Russian confrontation are at most a foretaste, not a full-scale reality, they nonetheless should serve, first, to challenge the notion that, in this tightly interconnected world, countries cannot slip back into the politics of the past and, second, to signal the grave but uncertain future the two countries are entering. Still, that leaves unclarified the distinctive character of the current US–Russian rivalry, its ramified effects, and its prospective life-cycle.

If employed with care and due respect for the obvious differences, the framework that offers not only the most subtle insights into this confrontation but also a standard for judging how serious it is is the earlier US–Soviet Cold War. What, however, was that? What did the phrase "cold war" mean? George Orwell usually gets the credit for using it first, in an October 1945 newspaper article. Two months earlier the United

States had dropped the atomic bomb on Hiroshima and Nagasaki, and he was reflecting on the convergence of two grim trends. Gradually, he argued, "the surface of the earth is being parceled off into three great empires, each self-contained and cut off from contact with the outer world, and each ruled, under one disguise or another, by a self-elected oligarchy" (Orwell, 1945). He counted the United States and its allies as one of those empires and China as potentially the third, but, when he speculated that the stalemate among the three may be leading to an "epoch as horribly stable as the slave empires of antiquity," he had the Soviet Union most in mind. The three, "unable to conquer one another . . . are likely to continue ruling the world between them, and it is difficult to see how the balance can be upset except by slow and unpredictable demographic changes." Technology's newest and most terrifying advance he saw as the intersecting trend, reinforcing "a state which was at once unconquerable and in a permanent state of 'cold war' with its neighbors." To the extent his original turn of phrase had content, it was in the remarkable insight with which he concluded the piece: the atomic bomb "is likeliest to put an end to large-scale wars at the cost of prolonging indefinitely a 'peace that is no peace.'"

Walter Lippmann, the dean of postwar American foreign policy writers, did the most to popularize the term in 1947, in a series of columns in the *New York Herald Tribune*, republished the same year as *The Cold War: A Study in US Foreign Policy since 1945*. Despite the book's title, Lippmann was concerned less with elaborating the features of this new phenomenon than with attacking the newly sketched US strategy for dealing with it. That summer, George Kennan's famous *Foreign Affairs* article making the case for the policy of "containment" had appeared, and Lippmann thought it a recipe for disaster – an approach that accepted an open-ended deadlock ceding the strategic advantage to the Soviet Union and for which the United States surely did not have the staying power. Instead, he argued, the United States should recognize the postwar landscape as an old-fashioned balance of power contest, with the Soviet Union as a reincarnation of an expansionist Imperial Russia, not some grandiose ideological apparition. The United States could not afford a dodge-and-parry strategy pursued inconclusively until who knew when the Soviet Union mutated or fell apart. The goal of the United States should be a political settlement that removed the Red Army back behind Soviet borders and blocked further Soviet expansion. To secure it, the United States should be willing to negotiate the withdrawal of its own forces from Europe. It was an idea that, ironically, Kennan entertained from the outset, and continued to argue for in the Reith Lectures delivered – to general disfavor – one decade later.

Once the term gained common currency, users felt some obligation to give it greater content. The result normally started from the obvious – that a cold war substituted for real war; that it was fought not through direct military action but indirectly though proxy wars, propaganda, witting and unwitting surrogates, and economic warfare. Stressing both its indirect rather than direct quality and the use of political and economic tools and tactics over the use of military force represented progress of sorts, but left things at such a high level of generality that the specific rhythms and peculiarities of the emerging contest slid by unobserved.

Later, some of the more useful commentary made the comparison to war itself. Michael Mandelbaum (2002) saw multiple similarities on several levels. "Like other major conflicts in the modern era," he wrote, "in the Cold War both sides deployed large armies and powerful arms in pursuit of incompatible goals." As in the twentieth century's great wars, "two powerful coalitions faced each other." As then, "its geographic scope was a wide one, indeed the widest of all, waged as it was across the entire planet and even extending into outer space." The two sides, as in the wars before, "mobilized the societies they governed." They "conscripted citizens into their armed forces and devoted appreciable parts of their national wealth, raised by taxation and borrowing, to the conflict." They devoted "scientific research and industrial technology to the manufacture of weaponry, leading . . . to arms races between the opposing coalitions."

Above all, Mandelbaum noted, the consequences of the two world wars and the Cold War were similar. "They changed everything: the hierarchy of power in the world, the location of borders, [and even] the character of regimes" because, at their close, "the government of the losing power fell, to be succeeded by one more like that of the winners." "Even the rules for relations between and among sovereign states" were transformed. From Mandelbaum's broad brush strokes, the Cold War begins to emerge as a large and compelling phenomenon with telling and distinctive features – although a few years later he might have wished to modify his judgment on how much the end of the Cold War had changed the character of the Russian regime – and, for that matter, the rules of international relations.

One arrives at this point, however, still without knowing what was unique about the Cold War, what separated it from the other previous forms of great power rivalry, and certainly without a basis for judging whether today's inflamed US–Russian relationship bears any resemblance to it. A deeper look into the Cold War experience is needed. What, after all, in its purest form was the Cold War? Call it the ideal version of the Cold War – the model itself. The Cold War came closest to this in its early phases, as the conflict escalated from the Berlin blockade in 1948 though the Korean War (1950–53) to the end of the Stalin era in 1953. During these years the confrontation most fully embodied qualities special to a cold war, qualities that lingered in subsequent years in attenuated but still potent form, until at the end they had weakened to near nothing.

First, if not unique to the Cold War then central to its inception, each side regarded the confrontation as exclusively the fault of the other side – not merely because of its behavior but, indeed, because of its very nature. The essence of the conflict was in the other side's essence. The interacting effects of the two sides' aims, fears, and actions did not enter the equation. Thus, by 1950 the Truman administration officially pronounced the Soviet Union as "unlike previous aspirants to hegemony . . . animated by a new fanatic faith, antithetical to our own," and determined "to impose its absolute authority over the rest of the world."[4] "No other value system," it continued, "is so wholly irreconcilable with ours, so implacable in its purpose to destroy ours, so capable of turning to its own uses the most dangerous and divisive trends in our own society, [and] no other so skillfully and powerfully evokes the elements of irrationality in human nature everywhere." Worse, "no other has the support of a great and growing center of military power."

If that sounded harsh and devoid of introspection, the Soviet perspective matched it. As World War II faded into the past, Stalin's lieutenant Andrei Zhdanov announced at the founding meeting of a new Communist International in September 1947 that the world was dividing "into two major camps" (Zhdanov, 1947). On one side was "the imperialist and anti-democratic camp," whose "cardinal purpose" was "to strengthen imperialism, to hatch a new imperialist war, to combat socialism and democracy, and to support reactionary and anti-democratic pro-fascist regimes and movements everywhere." On the other side stood "the anti-imperialist and democratic camp," led by the Soviet Union and "the new democracies" [his characterization of the Soviet Union's new Eastern European satellites]. "The purpose of this camp," he declared, was "to resist the threat of new wars and imperialist expansion, to strengthen democracy, and to extirpate the vestiges of fascism."

Second, because for both sides the Cold War was not merely over conflicting interests but, at root, over conflicting purposes, in the early phases neither much believed in looking for common ground. Any agreement, their instincts told them, would inevitably be "your gain is my loss," not mutually rewarding. In the famous *Foreign Affairs* article laying out the concept of containment, George Kennan wrote, "there can never be on Moscow's side any sincere assumption of a community of aims" between the Soviet Union and the capitalist adversary. "If the Soviet Government occasionally sets its signature to documents which would indicate the contrary, this is to be regarded as a tactical maneuver permissible in dealing with the enemy (who is without honor) and should be taken in the spirit of *caveat emptor*" (Kennan, 1947). Even when, a decade and a half into the Cold War, this wariness eased enough to allow for meaningful agreement, such as the nuclear test ban in 1963, neither party thought of it as anything other than a step to manage a competition that could not be overcome.

Third, both countries operated with the assumption that the contest could end only with either a fundamental change in the other side or its collapse. On the US side, NSC 68, the 1950 national security strategy, warned that "the intensifying struggle requires us to face the fact that we can expect no lasting abatement of the crisis unless and until a change occurs in the nature of the Soviet system." On the Soviet side, Stalin, in his last ideological foray, insisted that the law of the "inevitability of war among capitalist states" remained in place – notwithstanding the advent of nuclear weapons or the chance that the peace movement could halt the slide toward war in the near-term (Stalin, 1952). World War II, Soviet doctrine had it, was the dictum's latest proof. "To eliminate the inevitability of war," Stalin affirmed, "it is necessary to abolish imperialism."

Fourth, in the rare instances where momentary agreement might be contemplated, this could only be one-off and tactical, not a step leading to further agreements. Neither leadership cared – or dared – to believe that accord in one area could ease the obstacles to accord in others. Hence, any thought that, by a slow accumulation of even limited agreements, a process might emerge transforming the relationship simply did not enter people's minds.

And, fifth, while areas of temporary cooperation remained highly compartmentalized, areas of conflict did not. From the start, trouble in one area metastasized to others. Tension over Moscow's subjugation of Czechoslovakia in early 1948 translated into still greater tension over trends in postwar Germany and, in summer, to the first direct East–West military confrontation triggered by the Soviet-imposed Berlin blockade. The cascade of aggressive Soviet moves in Eastern Europe merged in the minds of Western leaders with Moscow's seeming determination to undo arrangements over the divided Germany. When, combined with what were viewed as Soviet covetous designs on Iran's northern province and readiness to promote violent change in Greece and Turkey, images converged, the United States joined what were about to become European allies in turning the modest Treaty of Brussels into the NATO alliance. In short order the Cold War had been militarized. A year later the Korean War, viewed by many Western capitals as a backdoor assault on Western security with direct implications for the standoff in Europe, produced a frenzied effort to put teeth into the alliance.

Nor for the Soviet Union, notwithstanding the predatory character of many of its actions, was the tumult of events in these years less of an ominous mosaic. Whatever double-dealing in Eastern Europe it thought the United States and Great Britain were engaged in, it viewed the changes they were making in "bizonia," their spheres in a newly divided Germany, as directed expressly against Soviet interests. The link from there to the formation of an openly anti-Soviet military alliance, combined with secret US efforts to organize guerrilla groups within the Soviet Union, flowed into a large, shapeless pool of suspicion and mounting hostility. It culminated in the grimmest of reactions: in fall 1950, at the height of the Korean War, Stalin, in a letter to Kim Il Sung (he was trying to persuade the Korean leader to pressure China to send troops into the war) wrote, "if a war is inevitable then let it be waged now, and not in a few years when Japanese militarism will be restored as an ally of the USA, and when the USA and Japan will have a ready-made bridgehead on the continent in the form of entire Korea run by Syngman Rhee" (Stalin, 1950).

The New Cold War

If the notion of cold war can legitimately be applied to the recent dramatic deterioration in Russia's relations with the United States specifically and with the West more broadly, it is because all of these qualities are present. Once more, as in the early years of the original Cold War, both sides see fault only in the other side. In February 2015, Vice-President Joseph Biden appeared at the Munich conference where six years earlier he had announced the newly elected Obama administration's desire to "reset" a tattered US–Russian relationship, only this time bearing a very different message (Biden, 2015b): "All of us," he said, had hoped for a Russia "more prosperous, more invested in the international order." To that end the United States had supported the creation of the NATO–Russia Council and "Russian membership in countless other institutions." But "unfortunately," he continued, "President Putin has chosen a different path." He has taken the path of "increased repression at home," including the use of "psychiatric institutions to quell dissent," shown "contempt for the rights of Russia's neighbors to choose their own future," disrespected "the sovereign, territorial integrity of Ukraine," as well as that of Georgia and Moldova, and disregarded commitments "made in Helsinki, Paris, Budapest."

A few months before, Putin made plain that he also saw a single culprit. The United States, full of itself for having "won the Cold War," he told the Valdai Discussion Club in October 2014, chose not to maintain global "order and stability," but instead "took steps that threw the system into sharp and deep imbalance" (Putin, 2014b). Those who refused to submit, he said, end up the victims of the "use of force, economic and propaganda pressure, meddling in domestic affairs, and appeals to a kind of 'supra-legal' legitimacy when they need to justify illegal intervention in this or that conflict or toppling inconvenient regimes." Washington may think that its "meddling in events all around the world is bringing peace, prosperity, progress, growth, and democracy," but, in fact, "unilateral diktat" escalates conflicts, spreads "chaos" rather than producing "sovereign and stable states," and, "instead of democracy," swells the ranks of malefactors, from "open neo-fascists to Islamic radicals."

"I don't want to psychoanalyze Mr. Putin," Obama responded, but "I will say that he has a foot very much in the Soviet past" (Obama, 2015). The course he had set for Russia was running the country into the ground, and that was bad not only for Russia but also for the United States because, "if Russia is doing badly, the concern is that they revert to old expansionist ideas that shouldn't have any application in the 21st century." And so it went. If one searched for a leader, policymaker, or politician on either side who included somewhere in her or his analysis thoughts about missteps or failings on both sides, the quest would have been in vain.

What made the parallel with the early years of the original Cold War more complete, however, was the unrelenting repetition of the same themes, only in shriller form, by politicians and the media. Television viewers tuned into Fox TV on an early day in November 2014 would have heard the columnist George Will say that Putin "is like Hitler" and, like him, has a grievance. Hitler's was over the Versailles Treaty and the humiliation of the World War I settlement (Will, 2014). Putin's is "against NATO, which was the architect of what he calls the great geopolitical tragedy of the 20th century." "Compared to Putin playing with his nuclear forces, the Islamic State is child's play." To finish, Will intoned, "frankly, the Ukraine is merely the appetizer . . . he does want to destroy NATO. And the way to do that is to take a bite out of one of the Baltic States and watch" NATO security guarantees "be ignored," which Will had "complete confidence" they would be.

In Russia, public commentary more than matched the harshest invective heard in the United States, and, because it was orchestrated by those at the top, it seemed all the more unyielding. On Russian television, day after day, program after program, US responsibility for virtually everything gone wrong in the world constituted a steady drumbeat. The United States, unsurprisingly, given the charges leveled by Russian officials, was condemned for spreading chaos in and around the Middle East, energizing Islamist terrorism, and plotting the street violence that launched the Ukrainian crisis. More surprisingly, however, it was accused by various media speakers of being behind the Hong Kong riots in October 2014 and the attack on the French satirical journal *Charlie Hebdo* in January 2015, and some of the more unhinged even suggested that US "special services" may have engineered the murder of the Russian opposition politician Boris Nemtsov in February 2015.

Even moderate voices attached blame primarily to the other side. In the 2014 Trilateral Commission report on Russia, the North American – principally US – authors began their chapter with the terse observation that, after Russia's aggression in Ukraine, "Washington accepted that Russia, at least under Vladimir Putin, is an adversary bent on pursuing regional hegemony and challenging the western-led international system. Twenty-five years after the fall of the Berlin Wall, containment is back." Strobe Talbott, one of the country's most sensitive and respected students of Russia, in a lecture in August 2014, painted Putin as a throwback to Russia's antediluvian past who has turned his back on "Russia's European vocation and embraced the Eurasian option," who uses irritants in the US–Russian relationship "as confirmations of his own combative, paranoid worldview," and, as a result, whose Russia is now "an immediate threat to its neighbors, a disruptive and divisive force in the evolution of Europe, and a potential threat to world peace" (Talbott, 2014).

Meanwhile their Russian counterparts ceded nothing to the Americans when fixing responsibility on the other side. One of the most prominent, Sergei Karaganov, pronounced his verdict: "While proclaiming a policy aimed at supporting peace and stability," the United States was, in fact, "transitioning to a policy of de-stabilizing key regions of the world" (Karaganov, 2014b). Worse, the United States and its European allies, he argued in another piece, had become "a directionless gaggle, beset with economic insecurities and losing sight of its moral convictions" (Karaganov, 2014a). Where Karaganov treated US culpability mockingly, and bravely asserted the advantages that a recharged Russia had in the new contest, others were far more scathing. Obama, one wrote, lists Russia as a major threat, after the Islamic State and before the Ebola contagion. "They equate us to a contemptible, small, deadly virus in order to declare Russia a sanitary cordon to be isolated and pitilessly exterminated" (Solozobov, 2014).

Alternative perspectives were not entirely missing. There were some who acknowledged that mistakes had been made on both sides, but these contrary voices floated helplessly amid hurricane-force winds.[5] Among Russian observers, any suggestion, even by the well placed, that Russia bore some responsibility for the destructive spiral came wrapped in cotton, conspicuously devoid of specifics. Thus, Igor Ivanov, Putin's first foreign minister and someone deeply distressed by the turn relations between the two countries had taken, detailed the many missteps by the United States, from NATO enlargement to the abrogation of the Anti-Ballistic Missile Treaty in 2001, the war in Iraq in 2003, the support for "color revolutions" in 2003 and 2004, and the general disregard of international law, but, as for Russia, he left it at "this rather depressing list can be continued as well" with "the list of Russia's steps towards the West." None was identified (Ivanov, 2014).

The original Cold War's second quality – the conviction that it was not worth struggling to find common ground, because conflicting purposes rather than merely conflicting interests divided the two sides – also applied once again. In the 1990s, the United States and Russia had their disagreements over many issues, not just concerning NATO enlargement and the 1999 Kosovo War, but over the Russian sale of cryogenic technology to India's space program, the delayed withdrawal of Russian troops from the Baltic states, Russia's involvement with Iran's Bushehr nuclear reactor, and the US handling of the Bosnian conflict. Always, however, leaders on both sides treated these conflicting interests as just that, and then, from the South Lawn of the White House or St Catherine's Hall in the Kremlin, solemnly repeated their common responsibility as the two dominant nuclear powers for global peace and stability.

No longer. Conflicting interests are now treated as but the surface manifestation of alien purpose. The Russian leadership portrays the Obama administration not merely as misguided but as doggedly determined to preserve a special role for itself – one allowing it to dictate to others, use force as it chooses, and ride roughshod over international rules and institutions. As part of its aggressive agenda, the United States is dead set on limiting and, where possible, rolling back Russian influence and, ultimately, bringing down the Putin regime. Indeed, say Russian officials, such is the real objective of the harsh sanctions regime the administration has orchestrated. More specifically, as will be explored in chapter 3, Putin and those around him have convinced themselves that the United States has a formal strategy of regime change, and, for more than a decade, whenever and wherever it served its purpose, the US has intervened with force, promoted "color revolutions," or instigated *coups d'état* to implement it. What it has done and is doing in Ukraine is simply its latest and most dangerous installment. By this reading, the threat posed by the United States transcends the prospect of a hostile Ukraine gravitating toward NATO. In its gravest form it is an existential threat to the Russian regime itself and, by extension, to the Russian state.

Viewed from the other side of the divide, a troubled Russia under increasingly authoritarian rule has allegedly cast aside whatever ambivalent interest it may once have had in working together on European security, decided that it will write its own rules, and set about forcibly redrawing the map to its taste, even if this has meant destabilizing its neighbors and upending the postwar European order. To make matters worse, for many in the Obama administration, most of the Congress, and much of the media, Russia's malign purpose has an incorrigible source: the system Putin and his allies have built requires it. The system needs external enemies – hence, the anti-Americanism. The system fears the infectious effects from democracy on its borders – hence, the determination to prevent it from growing within Ukraine. The system risks losing legitimacy in the eyes of the Russian public if it fails to deliver economically – hence, the search for alternative sources of legitimacy, such as the chauvinism stirred by the annexation of Crimea.

The third characteristic of the original Cold War is again also present, although in a less primal form. Just as before, leaders on both sides have reconciled themselves to no basic change in the relationship as long as leadership on the other side – or leadership like it – remains in place. True, because this pessimism is less rooted in warring ideologies – ideologies premised on a fundamental incompatibility of political and economic systems – the time frame in people's minds appears to be less forbidding. Leadership could change, and, even if the precise probability of this happening remains unclear, the hope has greater immediacy and credibility for them than it did for their predecessors during the earlier confrontation.

Fourth, as in the original Cold War, particularly its early phases, neither side wastes much time imagining that future elements of cooperation could become cumulative and gradually, step by step, transform the relationship into something more positive. Cooperation, rare in any case, it is assumed, will be only "transactional," not transformational. On a few specific issues where sheer practicality encourages a joint effort, the transaction may be done, but with no expectation that anything else will follow, any more than that one's purchase of a pair of shoes implies ever more elaborate commercial ties.

A harbinger of this attitude on the US side had emerged nearly a decade ago, even before the 2008 Russian war in Georgia, even before

Putin's ferocious attack on US foreign policy at the 2007 Munich Security Conference. In 2006, a Council on Foreign Relations task force, reacting to the clouds already forming in the relationship, argued that the most the United States should strive for was "selective cooperation" (Edwards and Kemp, 2006). "The mutual confidence that partnership requires is missing." Hence, the report contended, "When Russia and the United States work together it is likely to be a matter of case-by-case, carefully circumscribed cooperation." And then, to anticipate the assumption underlying this proposition, the report's authors stressed that "cooperation in one case does not necessarily make cooperation in the next more likely." Yet, even they did not envisage a relationship as denuded of cooperation on major issues as today's. On the contrary, while they stressed the need to lower expectations and balance the desire for cooperation with a tough-minded approach to the very real differences existing between the two countries, they clearly did not doubt the need for or the feasibility of the United States and Russia addressing together nuclear arms control, the spread of weapons of mass destruction (WMD), energy security, and the threat from terrorism.

Finally, the fifth feature of the original Cold War also echoes in the US–Russian confrontation of our day. As then, tensions in one area of the relationship have inexorably contaminated nearly all others. Leaders in both countries insist that important areas of cooperation remain untouched by the schism, and they have a point. Both sides continue to implement the 2010 New START agreement. They worked together in producing the tentative nuclear agreement with Iran. Until May 2015, Moscow permitted a route across Russia for US and NATO forces withdrawing from Afghanistan. And they have kept in place collaboration key to the US space program. All of this is important, but to take these lingering instances of cooperation as proof that things are not as bad as they seem, or that even they are not endangered, would be an illusion.

In fact, on a wide range of subjects where the two governments had been talking and several where progress had been made, the talking has stopped and the progress has been lost. Like falling dominoes, each has given way as the shock waves from the Ukraine crisis rippled outward. Some of these were out of view but consequential, such as the increasingly ambitious program of military exchanges developed by the military leadership on the two sides and projects to promote energy efficiency, such as smart (electric) grids, the use of energy performance contracts, and the development of clean energy in Russia's Far East. Others were more high profile, storied, and critical in the larger scheme of things, such as the prospect of advancing from New START to the next step in strategic arms control, a prospect that has now vanished, or the chance to turn US plans to develop missile defense from a source of competition into a basis of cooperation, which also has disappeared.

The contagion showed most clearly where, historically, relations had been most cooperative. Going back to the Soviet period, the two countries had always labored together to constrain the risks of nuclear proliferation. Beyond the 1968 Treaty on the Non-Proliferation of Nuclear Weapons (NPT), one of the most important and successful efforts had been the Cooperative Threat Reduction program (CTR), known more commonly as the Nunn–Lugar Act, named for the two senators, Sam Nunn and Richard Lugar, who conceived and shepherded it through Congress. Over the quarter century of its existence, it played the key role in removing nuclear weapons from Belarus, Kazakhstan, and Ukraine, decommissioning nuclear, biological, and chemical weapons in Russia, and securing weapons-grade nuclear materials throughout the former Soviet Union. In December 2014, nine months into the Ukrainian crisis, Russian officials informed their US counterparts that they were ending it. Two months earlier, Moscow announced that it would not attend the 2016 Nuclear Security Summit. This has been a major initiative of the Obama administration, central to its efforts to rally the international community behind stronger safeguards on fissile material, and a conference Russia had attended three times before. And in the ill-fated 2015 NPT Review Conference, while the main clash dooming the outcome was between the nuclear-weapons states (including the United States and Russia) and those states not possessing nuclear weapons, the two lined up against each other on scheduling a conference to establish a WMD-free zone in the Middle East, the specific issue that torpedoed a final document.

Why it Cannot Be a Cold War

Still, do not the fundamental differences between the original Cold War and contemporary US–Russian relations, bad as they may be, disqualify the comparison? After all, the Cold War lasted half a century, and the current imbroglio has been underway scarcely more than a year. Duration, however, is not the critical criterion. If the markings are there, that is enough. Cancer is cancer, whether the struggle is won quickly or the battle is long. But are the markings there in this case?

In key respects, many would say they are not. First, whatever it is, the confrontation between Russia and the United States plus the Europeans is not the ordering principle for the global political setting. It is a new feature of contemporary international politics, not an all-encompassing factor dictating the international system's shape and dynamics. Second, distracting as the conflict is, it does not consume US and Russian foreign policy as it once did. Once, it was the core around which much of the rest of US and Soviet foreign policy revolved, not least because the proxy wars they waged reached to all corners of the world. Today, for both, it is one dimension – perhaps an enlarged dimension – in a foreign policy that has multiple dimensions.

Third, the world is a different place from what it was in the middle of the twentieth century, and Russia's place in it is more different still. An autarkic Soviet economy, with closed borders, and a shuttered population could isolate itself from the outside world and be isolated by the United States. Today the two countries cannot isolate themselves from each other, or for long refuse to engage, when their economies are enmeshed in global energy, capital, and technology markets; their societies exposed to the same threats from drugs, disease, terrorism, and other sources of disorder; and their people connected by the internet and informed by social media. Fourth, for all the flying sticks and spittle, the swelling hostility between them does not have the deep ideological animus of the Cold War. The United States may castigate the Russian leadership for trampling on democratic values, and Russia may condemn the United States for profaning traditional social values by tolerating same-sex marriage and celebrating crass materialism, but the rancor does not spring from battling notions of how the world works, nor is it underpinned by competing political and economic ideologies.

Finally, the threat of nuclear Armageddon does not loom menacingly over the relationship as it did during the Cold War – particularly during its tensest moments, such as the Berlin crises from 1958 through 1961, the Cuban missile crisis in 1962, and the October 1973 Yom Kippur War in the Middle East. The United States is not about to restore to public schools those yellow and black pinwheel signs that showed students where to go during a nuclear attack. And ABC has no plans to produce another film like *The Day After*, the 1983 television drama depicting what happened in Lawrence, Kansas, after NATO and the Warsaw Pact go to war and the nuclear missile silos in Kansas are wiped out (even if it remains the most watched television film in US history). Nor – at least not yet – are Russian authorities resuming the elaborate civil defense plans and drills given special attention during the early years of the first Reagan administration, when talk of nuclear war figured prominently in the media of both countries.

At one level all of this is quite true. The differences between then and now are obvious, and any suggestion that the new Russia–West Cold War duplicates the original would be nonsense. Considered more carefully, however, the contrast is less stark than at first glance. Thus, while the original Cold War did swell to affect nearly every dimension of international politics and every region of the world, the force driving it was a bilateral relationship. Had there been no US–Soviet contest, there would have been no Cold War; had that contest been less intense, so also would have been the Cold War.

The Cold War, therefore, had both a critical bilateral as well as a universal dimension. The alliance systems that formed and gave the Cold War its initial bipolar character radiated out from this bilateral core. And it was US and Soviet competition in all quarters of the globe – from Vietnam to Nicaragua, from the Middle East to South Africa – that propelled the Cold War forward and infused it with its defining quality.

Indeed, one need not think of cold war as only a generalized phenomenon. It can also characterize a poisoned bilateral relationship. What, after all, has been the nature of the US–Iranian relationship since the 1979 revolution other than cold war? How much wider and more profound will the damage be in the larger setting if the US–Russian relationship continues to harden into something similar. Thus, an alternative way to think about the subject starts not with the effects of a world frozen in a cold war, but with the effects on the world of two major players locked in a cold war. Those, as I am about to argue, can be grave indeed. And they can be grave even if the standoff does not represent the incubus for or motor behind another system-wide cold war.

Second, granted that, unlike their predecessors, neither US nor Russian leaders can afford to preoccupy themselves with the challenge that they believe the other side poses, this still leaves a good deal of room for the distorting effect that the new Cold War can have on the remainder of their foreign policy. They cannot but devote considerable energy to dealing with the trouble emanating from the Islamic south, the uncertain course of a rising China, and problems in their own back-yard. Yet, how and how well they deal with these and many of the other issues crowding their foreign policy agenda will be heavily influenced by the way their duel unfolds – almost certainly not for the better.

Third, the conviction that the world and Russia's place in it are too different to permit the renewal of cold war also deserves a bit more reflection. It may be that countries today are so tightly knitted together – their societies and economies so entwined – that anything approxi-mating the frictions and the face-offs of the decades after World War II is ruled out. But the last period of rapid growth in interdependence at the end of the nineteenth century, when the revolution in communica-tions and transportation destroyed the space dividing countries and melded their economies together, did not prevent the great powers from sliding back into a deadly political competition – in that case, with a disastrous end. The imagination, however, need not run to world war. Even the revival of a drawn-out strategic rivalry between two or more countries will be damaging enough, and, given the cur-rent state of US–Russian relations and their trajectory, it would take a cavalier mind to confidently predict that this time around the bonds of interdependence will not let it happen.

Moreover, perhaps it is best not to lean too heavily on the safe-guards and constraints a globalized world provides if, as a number of signs indicate, the process of globalization has slowed, even begun to reverse itself. What some call "de-globalization" may already have set in, and "our interconnected world" may be "shrinking back toward its national borders" (Kurlantzick, 2015). They point to shrinking volumes of trade, the sharp pull back of bank lending into emergent markets, the growth of protectionism in major economies, the slowing of cross-border migration (before the European migration crisis in fall 2015), and the impairing of social and cultural contacts.

Moreover, the most comprehensive survey, whose matrix incor-porates everything from trade to tourism, from portfolio and direct foreign investment to internet traffic, indicates that, whether meas-ured by *depth* (that is, as the ratio of international to domestic activity) or *breadth* (that is, the international portion of activity that travels beyond one or few neighboring countries), Russia comes out decid-edly low (Ghemawat and Altman, 2015). In terms of depth, Russia's global ranking is 101st out of a 140 countries, behind Cambodia, Mauritius, and Tajikistan. And, in terms of breadth, it is 48th, behind Ghana, the Philippines, and Sri Lanka. Added to this, in several areas – e.g., restricting the internet, limiting the role of transnational organizations, and commandeering national industry in the name of self-sufficiency – it has set a policy course promoting de-globalization.

As for the fourth objection – the absence of a deep ideological antipathy driving the confrontation – plausible substitutes exist. When in 1993 Samuel Huntington published his seminal article "The clash of civilizations?," arguing that "the fundamental source of conflict" in the new era "will be cultural," replacing what for 300 years had been the conflict, first, between princes, then between nation states, and ultimately between ideologies, many scoffed. His thesis, they said, was too crude, too indifferent to the many forces blurring the lines between civilizations – civilization itself being a dubious notion.[6]

Whether one agrees that the Slavic-Orthodox world constitutes a distinct civilization (one of Huntington's six major civilizations) or that religion constitutes its core element, let alone that it will be the primary fuel for conflict, one element in his definition does resonate: the role of national identity. In the original Cold War, for the United States and the Soviet Union, ideology constituted identity – at least in its early decades. Now, however, national identity derives more from factors shaping contemporary nationalism, such as social values, historical myth, and grievances against others. In Russia, the way these elements are fusing is very much in flux but currently trending toward an iden-tity alien to that of the United States – indeed, one, as Gilbert Rozman (2014) contends, in noticeable part built around "the demonization of the United States."

Finally, while the cloud of nuclear war mercifully does not hang over the relationship as it once did, thoughts of how it could re-form, inconceivable a year or two ago, no longer are. Officials on both sides now nervously talk of steps taken by the other side to make nuclear weapons more useable. They have begun again to treat the weap-ons programs of the other side as a cause for alarm and a threat that requires a direct response. And, in the Ukrainian crisis, they now have a real-world scenario that makes the path to a nuclear confrontation anything but an abstraction.

Why Care?

So, suppose that Russia and United States have veered into a new Cold War, that their brawl shares sufficient characteristics with the original one to justify the label. Does it really matter? This is not, after all, your grandmother's contest between two superpowers standing astride the international system, creating force fields sucking states caught between into battling alliances, and inflicting their struggle on nearly every international institution and into nearly everyone else's conflict. This, as has already been said, is not a contest between equals. Russia does not come close to posing the challenge to US policy that nine US presidents believed the Soviet Union did. As Obama dismissively put it early in the Ukrainian crisis: "Russia is a regional power that is threatening some of its immediate neighbors – not out of strength but out of weakness" (Wilson, 2014).

One wonders whether the president really meant it (or whether he was not simply countering Republican talk that Mitt Romney had been right when, during the 2012 presidential campaign, he had claimed that Russia "is our No. 1 geopolitical foe"). His disesteem scarcely squared with the view of William Burns, the high-level official in the Obama administration who began a 2009 speech with the "glaringly obvious." "Russia," he said, "matters" (Burns, 2009). "Few nations could make more of a difference to our success than Russia." And he then listed the ways. Nor did Obama in 2014 sound like Obama speaking to students in Moscow five years earlier, when he assured them that the United States wanted Russia to occupy "its rightful place as a great power" (Obama, 2009).

The difference between Burns's and, presumably, the president's views in 2009 and the way the administration felt compelled to frame the issue in 2014 underscores a basic problem. Burns's elaboration of how greatly and in what ways Russia mattered to the United States was a distinctly rare occasion. In the two decades since the collapse of the Soviet Union, US leaders had often uttered flattering phrases about Russia's importance, but without spelling out the reasons and, therefore, more importantly, without establishing for themselves, their administration, and the various constituencies whose support they needed what the stakes were. If that was true of the US side, it was truer yet on the Russian side.

Burns's acknowledgement was rare when compared not only with what had not come before but with what did not follow. As a result, having failed to recognize – or, at least, having failed to articulate – the stakes that each country had in the relationship, neither was in much of a position to appreciate (or be constrained by) what was being lost as the relationship disintegrated. If the concept of cold war helps not only to understand this new reality but to weigh its consequences, that is a second – and perhaps more important – justification for its use.

These begin with the obvious – nuclear weapons – but not in the obvious way that nuclear weapons usually figure in a discussion of US–Russian relations. The now banished hope of negotiating still smaller numbers of US and Russian nuclear warheads and delivery vehicles or generating support for a world without nuclear weapons, laudable as those measures would have been, pales in comparison to challenges in what is now a new era, the second nuclear age – challenges that a new US–Russia Cold War will guarantee go unattended.

The earlier nuclear era had the merit of featuring two nuclear super-powers that, after twice stumbling toward nuclear war, retreated and, in effect, agreed to rules giving their nuclear relationship a certain level of stability. That period is over, although thinking in Moscow and Washington has yet to move beyond it. The period we now enter has perils and a complexity vastly exceeding the earlier one and requiring approaches far more creative and varied than anything tried during the Cold War. These will need to be supple, attuned to the intricate geometry of a world with multiple nuclear actors, and open to a mix of formal and informal, negotiated and tacit arrangements.

The dangers begin with the direction new nuclear technologies are taking, such as the growing emphasis on precision-guided, often hypersonic, conventionally armed missiles capable of striking targets, including nuclear sites, anywhere in the world in less than an hour. The United States, Russia, and China are all at different stages in developing this technology, but all are busy doing so. If fully developed, the technology would allow a country to use conventional weapons to carry out attacks on another country's nuclear forces and, in the process, greatly weaken the firebreak between conventional and nuclear war. Similarly, the United States, China, and Russia, each nervously eyeing what the others may be doing or planning to do to put offensive weapons in space – that is, weapons capable of destroying objects in space or on land – are toying with options allowing them to go down this road.

Where unconstrained technology threatens to lead, however, is but the first level of a multi-tiered problem. For there are also the risks of catastrophe in unstable relationships between other nuclear powers – most notably India and Pakistan. One, Pakistan, is building shorter-range nuclear systems faster than nearly any other country, and, worse, evidently persuaded that in another conventional war with India, given India's clear-cut advantage, the Pakistani military could resort to battlefield or tactical nuclear weapons without risking escalation to all out nuclear war if these were used on Pakistani soil (Sankaran, 2015). The other, India, is speeding toward the world's third nuclear triad – that is, nuclear weapons deployed on land, in the sea, and in the air – and has now tested an intercontinental ballistic missile capable of reaching Beijing, creating a vastly more complicated triangular nuclear competition. Together India and Pakistan are moving to make the Indian Ocean an extension of their nuclear aspirations, India through its ambitious ballistic missile submarine program and

Pakistan "by dispersing low-yield nuclear weapons across a variety of naval platforms" (Rahman, 2015).

Trends in US-China military preoccupations with potential nuclear implications are equally ominous – and made more dangerous by the unwillingness of either country to face them. Matters originate in China's determination to extend its security perimeter out across the three China seas (the Yellow Sea, the East China Sea, and the South China Sea), and to do so by keeping at bay US naval forces viewed by Washington as critical to maintaining the defense of Japan and South Korea. The United States sees the threat, to use the jargon of the Pentagon, as one of "anti-access/area denial" (A2/AD), and its answer is a strategy known as "air-sea battle," which, in the event of conflict, anticipates pre-emptively striking the Chinese mainland and the cruise missiles and aircraft that the Chinese would use against US aircraft carrier forces. Some within the US Air Force even justify potential nuclear-tipped long-range cruise missiles as useful in blowing a hole in Chinese air defenses, allowing US stealth aircraft to complete their mission (Kristensen, 2014).

This is but one, admittedly worrying, element among many contributing to a US-China nuclear arms competition, and that competition is but one element in a dangerously complex nuclear world that desperately needs conscious efforts to bring some level of order and stability to it. While any such effort will require collaboration among multiple states – none more important than China – leadership can come only from the two countries with 92 percent of the world's nuclear weapons. If earlier the prospect of such leadership was less than promising, the effect of the new US-Russia Cold War has been to rule it out entirely.

Worse, the new Cold War is giving a powerful impetus to the collapse of the arms control regime slowly and painfully assembled over the last half century. The treaty regulating missile defense systems died a decade and half ago, but now the 1987 treaty banning US and Russian intermediate-range nuclear missiles (INF) is in danger of following suit. Talk of finding a replacement for the moribund treaty regulating conventional military forces in Europe has ended, and so too has any thought of moving forward with treaties to limit the production of fissile material and end nuclear testing in all atmospheres. Earlier Russian reluctance to discuss limits on sub-strategic (or tactical) nuclear weapons has turned into a stone-faced dismissal of the very idea – not least because the Russian military has made them an important element in military planning. Any hope of moving to the next stage of US–Russian strategic nuclear arms reductions has been paralyzed, and increasingly the task is to save the 2010 New START agreement. And scarcely any of the planned steps intended to strengthen the nuclear non-proliferation treaty have been implemented, creating the inauspicious lead-up to and then failures at the 2015 five-year review conference.

Again, the argument is not that all was well on the arms control front in the years before US–Russian relations went over the edge. Parts of the scaffolding had already come loose and other parts remained uncompleted (Mecklin, 2015). But the future remained ambiguous, and in the ambiguity there existed hope. That is now gone, as one door after another slams shut.

The same can be said of the new and suddenly looming issue of cyber-security. Three countries – China, Russia, and the United States – are crucial where the spectrum of cyber threats shades into its most dangerous form: cyber-warfare – that is, the capacity to attack another country's vital infrastructure (air control systems, water supply, electric grids, and communications networks). In June 2013, in Northern Ireland, on the sidelines of the last summit before the G-8 again became the G-7, Obama and Putin agreed to begin cooperating on measures to increase transparency, confidence-building steps, and the exchange of cyber-security information. It was a baby step forward, but now it too has been halted, and, as the new Cold War deepens, almost certainly a further casualty will be any chance that the two countries return to the task of reining in the perils on war's new frontier.

Or take the damage that will likely be done on another critical new frontier: developing the Arctic region's rich hydrocarbon reserves. Harvesting the gas (30 percent of the world's undiscovered reserves) and oil (13 percent of the world's undiscovered reserves) poses enormous technological, ecological, and sociological challenges accompanied by unresolved legal disputes, but, to this point, the five Arctic littoral claimants have approached them in largely cooperative fashion. As virgin territory, unburdened by historical quarrels, the Arctic could have been an important piece contributing to the Euro-Atlantic security community that leaders on all sides have sworn they wanted to create throughout the post-Cold War period (EASI Energy, 2012). Instead, as part of the new Cold War, the economic sanctions the United States and its Western allies have imposed on Russia have the effect of blocking the joint development of these resources. At the same time, steps that different countries have taken to protect their interests militarily have suddenly emerged center stage. Russia, in particular, having already adjusted its force deployments and military doctrine for the Arctic, has begun to mount major military exercises linking preparations for conflict in Europe with ensuring "Russia's military security in the Arctic region" (Varandani, 2015).

The list of the ways hostile US–Russian relations will cripple efforts to come to grips with the twenty-first century's new challenges is much longer. Climate change and the resource conflicts bound to follow, if they are to be mitigated, will require leadership from the United States, Russia, and China, three of the four largest greenhouse gas emitters.

Each can contribute on its own, and the incipient US–Chinese cooperation now underway is important, but for real progress to be achieved the cooperation must be three-way, and the freeze in US–Russian relations promises that this will not happen. Nor will the noxious effects from the illicit flows of counterfeited goods, trafficked humans, endangered species, laundered money, and illegal arms be stemmed unless China and Russia, by far the two greatest offenders, become part of the solution. The prospect that either – least of all Russia – will be open to US entreaties to begin cracking down on this scourge, or that the United States will even bother to try, also fades into fantasy. Even something as sensible and non-political as US–Russian cooperation in developing vaccines and treatments for future Ebola-like epidemics – an area where both countries have special capacities – is also likely to fall victim.

These are opportunity costs – prohibitively expensive lost opportunities. One baleful consequence of the new Cold War, however, has no such wistful side to it. It is sheer unmediated tragedy – all the more so because it has so suddenly and so unexpectedly upended a reality on which all had counted. Amid the turmoil in other parts of the world, Europe appeared to be an anchor of stability. Tensions existed and on the margins violence occurred, but Europe seemed safely past its history as the crucible of great power conflict. The vast military forces poised against one another along Europe's dividing line during the Cold War had been substantially dismantled, as one alliance collapsed and the other shifted its attention elsewhere. While the desultory effort to underwrite the de-militarization of the new fault line between NATO and Russia with a modernized arms control regime had faltered, few any longer worried that the two sides would, in a dramatic turn, remilitarize their relationship, point re-energized military forces at one another, and face off across Europe's central front.

The crisis in Ukraine, beginning with Russia's annexation of Crimea and its role in the Donbas war, tripped the wire, and the two sides have rushed back to the familiar posture of preparing to fight each other, only this time, and in contrast to the situation in the last decades of the original Cold War, they are acting out of a sense of immediacy. Among NATO members a genuine nervousness exists that Russia may not stop with whatever its objectives are in Ukraine but boldly strike against NATO itself, say, by testing its security guarantees in the Baltic region. Among Russians the fear grows that the United States has seized on the Ukrainian crisis to reconstitute its military power on Russia's border and ready itself and NATO to strike Russia were further instability elsewhere in the region to provide a pretext. Each side has begun beefing up its capabilities where the two sides meet face to face. Each side has rapidly expanded the cat-and-mouse game of probing the other side's defense preparations and reaction times. And each side has mounted exercises expressly designed for war anywhere along a line from the Baltic to the Crimea (Frear et al., 2015). In the case of Russia, these exercises have involved the forward deployment of aircraft and missiles with nuclear payloads (Belfast Telegraph, 2015).

Hence the ongoing Ukrainian crisis, with its continuing risk of escalation, is a large, menacing part of a far graver problem. At the very heart of the new Russia–West Cold War, Russia, the United States, and its NATO allies are returning to the defining feature of the original Cold War: a militarized standoff over the future of a divided Europe. This time it has been moved to the East, to the edge of the former Soviet Union, and in more fraught circumstances, because the contested zone - the new lands between - is politically volatile and suspended between the two sides, not divided between them.

The new confrontation in Europe may be the new Cold War's clearest and most alarming manifestation, but, if for the foreseeable future, perhaps even for years, the United States and Russia remain on the current path, if beyond the Ukrainian crisis their enmity endures, as it is now set to do, the damage to each country's foreign policy and to the health of the international system will be far greater than leaders on either side have yet admitted. For the simple truth is that, on the major issues of international politics where US-Russian cooperation is essential, the prospect of achieving it is bleaker than at any time since the harsher periods of the original Cold War. That should be reason enough to look back at the earlier era, at what we now know of it, and, in particular, at what we can learn from it.

2

The Cold War

Epic historical eras fade very slowly. Their effects persist long after the period in which they occur. Even longer do historians argue over their causes, essence, and significance. If such was true of the Thirty Years War – the series of wars that devastated Europe between 1618 and 1648, fought first over religion, then among great powers emerging from the detritus of the Holy Roman Empire, and ending in the 1648 Peace of Westphalia, the charter that has guided international relations down to our own day – then one should not be surprised if the same holds true for the fifty-year Cold War.

For a generation born in the quarter century since the Cold War ended, however, those years have little meaning or even an identifiable shape; and so too for many who lived during the Cold War but for whom it is a faded memory, worlds away from what the morning newspaper or social media report. Looking back at the half century following World War II, let alone arguing over it, seems neither compelling nor particularly practical. Even if over this period leaders in Moscow and Washington subordinated almost everything they did to the contest they imagined they were in, and that contest flowed into almost every crack in the international system; even if, in the Berlin crises from 1958 to 1961, the Cuban missile crisis in 1962, and the Arab–Israeli War in 1973, they edged toward nuclear war; even if, with a wary eye to the moves of the other side, they inserted themselves into every war from Suez to Vietnam, from Angola to Afghanistan (twice), and from Gaza to Nicaragua; and even if they spent more than $25 trillion arming themselves and amassed more than 70,000 nuclear warheads, isn't it all history?

History it is, say the historians, but understanding that era better, correcting the misimpressions that we had living through it, and putting it all in perspective is more than intellectual aerobics. Beyond the virtue of knowing the thing in itself – that is, appreciating an important interlude in the human experience accurately and on its own terms – any important historical era has a legacy and offers important lessons. In this chapter and the two to follow I want to think about both. First, however, because interpreting the Cold War is a contentious matter, I start there. As the musty boxes of the archives open, the arguments mount – arguments over when it began and when it ended; over who bore more responsibility for it; over missed opportunities or not; and, above all, over why things happened as they did.

Weighing in on these arguments, however, is not the objective here. Better that they be used to shed light on the current course of events and to provide another angle allowing us to get outside the din of the moment and put today's confrontation in larger perspective. Thus, the issue is which of these arguments help do this – which offer insights that a straightforward look at what is occurring between the two countries does not and which wrestle with critical parts of a story that participants in today's story have not begun to contemplate. Hence, the perspective is reversed from chapter 1's concern with applying the concept of cold war to the currently mutilated state of US–Russian relations, and in this chapter the objective is to see what the original Cold War can teach us about the new Cold War.

Perceiving the Cold War

At this remove, were one to try to get, so to speak, outside the skin of the Cold War - to place it within the larger scheme of things in its day - two perspectives, both of them open to debate, force the discussion on to a higher plane. The first focuses on what historians, particularly in the French *Annales* school, call the *longue durée*. Fernand Braudel, the most famous modern exponent of this approach, viewed history as unfolding on three levels: the deep, glacial evolution of the physical environment; the slow but powerful force of long-term social, economic, and cultural change; and the more tangible effect of events. Events, the bricks and mortar of history, are man-made, the product of human choice, and they compose history as we experience it and then most commonly think of it. Meanwhile history at this level - for example, the Cold War's crises and accommodations - flows within canyons carved by the deeper, impersonal force of underlying historical trends.

Thought of in these terms, the Cold War, whatever its specific causes and pathways, was ultimately no match for the more powerful, slow, often interrupted but inexorable advance of liberal political and economic ideas and structures underway since the late eighteenth century. Francis Fukuyama, the argument's most famous herald, in his book *The End of History and the Last Man*, argued that, while the underlying historical narrative might in the future be momentarily disrupted by other dark detours, the outcome of the Cold War signaled the ultimate triumph of liberal democracy. Michael Mandelbaum, also writing in the fresh, warm breeze at the Cold War's end, agreed that the deeper pattern of history had surfaced and, for now and the foreseeable future, the ideas of Woodrow Wilson - peace (over war), democracy (over tyranny), and free markets (over economic diktat) - would prevail (Mandelbaum, 2002).

If history at the level of the *longue durée* has willed the inescapable superiority of liberal over illiberal outcomes, then the detour that
US–Russian relations are now taking has both a limited timeframe and
a likely destination. But what, say the critics, if history's deep under-
currents do not favor the liberal outcome but leave it contested by the
counter-currents of tyranny and the ever present possibility of war?
Or, even if one believes that the curve of history tilts toward a safer
and more democratic world, how long and painful may the interludes
of instability and confrontation be? At this deeper level the new US–
Russian Cold War may, indeed, make no sense. That, however, raises
no barrier to its existence, although with luck it may be relevant to its
end, assuming leaders on both sides stop long enough to reflect on
where they are headed.

If the first perspective features the Cold War's relationship to the
forces of history, a second concentrates on its relationship to political
context. Through much of the Cold War no one questioned whether
the international system and the Cold War were one and the same. The
international system was a bipolar one, and that was assumed to be
the other side of the Cold War coin. It makes a considerable difference,
however, if the two are not coterminous – if, for example, they do not
begin or end at the same time, or if a bipolar system need not produce
a cold war or a cold war can occur in other than bipolar systems. While
historians disagree over when the Cold War began and when it ended,
the range is sufficiently different from the timing assigned to the emergence and dissolution of the postwar international system that they
appear to be separate things.

True, a system dominated by two juxtaposed camps would seem
to have a natural tendency to end in cold war. Were the amorphous
polarity of the current international system to precipitate into a clearer
bipolarity between the United States and China, odds are that a cold

war would follow, and for reasons that Zbigniew Brzezinski once offered to explain the Cold War. "Two great powers," he wrote, "differentiated by divergent centuries-long experience and separated by sharply differing ideological perspectives, yet thrust into political proximity as a consequence of the shattering of the earlier international system, could hardly avoid being plunged into a competitive relationship" (Brzezinski, 1972). Hence, in contrast to explanations that focus on "human error and evil" or on key actors, he saw the Cold War as the "product of lengthy and probably ineluctable historical forces." It was "less a matter of Stalin or of Dulles and more of de Tocqueville."

To that extent, there was a logic to it. Bipolarity created that logic. A world whose structure comes in more colors and crowns more players who can make a difference does not have that logic. Today's world is distinctly multicolored, and presumably, whatever the factors driving the new US–Russian Cold War, the earlier "ineluctable historical forces" are not among them. In this world other logics ought to be at work, driven by a different set of historical forces, some of which, such as the new threats to global security, may, in fact, militate against the new Cold War and help to put brakes on it.

Conceiving the Cold War

Like any large, complex phenomenon, there are multiple ways to understand the Cold War. Two, however, help better than others to unscramble the tangle of interpretations vying to explain the new Cold War. The first is the venerable and widely accepted conviction that the Cold War was a battle between political and economic systems, underpinned by fundamentally different values, goals, and ontologies. Within this argument the principal contention was over the latter, over the ideological element, and whether it played a primary or secondary causal role. Less conspicuously, a second area of disagreement eventually emerged related to the primary sphere within which the inter-systemic rivalry took place. Scholars looking back over the whole of the Cold War charged that mainstream analysts, particularly international relations theorists, had gotten it wrong by stamping it Euro-centric – that is, as a strategic contest between the United States and the Soviet Union over the fate of the international system's European fulcrum – when, in fact, the Cold War's active theater was the Third World (Westad, 2007).

If the Cold War, as Fred Halliday (1999) argued, was as much a socio-economic contest for the hearts and minds of much of the globe as an ideological and geopolitical test of wills, then the fluid environment where it raged and, indeed, the point from which it ricocheted back into the anxiety-ridden consciousness of US and Soviet leaders was the vast expanses of a roiling postcolonial world. Halliday, to put a fine point on it, suggested that US "national security doctrines – from Truman to Reagan – were less about responding to Soviet geopolitical maneuvering and more concerned with responding to the geopolitical consequences of localized revolutionary crises" (Saull, 2011).

That was inside the argument. Outside of it, the opposing school insisted that the clash of political and economic systems mattered less than a simple, classical slugfest over power. The clash was merely the tissue covering the real muscle controlling events. Beginning with this elemental argument, all of these contested byways echo today. Thus, some argue that the trouble traces back to the wildly different assumptions motivating the two sides. From the Western perspective, everything begins with the red in tooth and claw determination of Russian leaders to reverse the loss of place and power following the collapse of the Soviet Union. From a Russian perspective, the root cause is in the (unexplained) determination of US leaders to diminish Russia and put it in a box. It is a simple struggle for power, and these are its terms.

Others, however, suspect that US–Russian tensions are about more than geopolitical transgressions and grudges; that value-laden notions of the good and right way to organize society are also creeping in. While the unraveling of relations did not originate in a competition over political-economic models, something akin had begun to take shape several years before the Ukrainian crisis drove relations over the cliff. As the Putin leadership tightened its political grip within Russia and moved to assert the state's control over the commanding heights of the economy, it increasingly identified with countries – first and foremost China – seen as pioneering authoritarian capitalism as an alternative to liberal capitalism. For the Russian regime, this new version of competing systems served both as self-justification and as the basis for arguing that authoritarian capitalism was now outpacing the West's increasingly defunct liberal model.

Back inside the argument, the disagreement over which sphere drove the Cold War also has a counterpart today, although it is not articulated as such. And, just as in the original case, the argument is not simply over the location of a confrontation but over the nature of that confrontation. Thus, for some, the core of the trouble between the United States and Russia – and more broadly between Russia and Europe – centers on the tug of war over the fate of countries on Russia's European border. Once relations move into the larger world, while there are frictions, the common interests that Russia shares with the West (preventing a nuclear-armed Iran, cooperating in the wind-down of the Afghan war, constraining the proliferation of nuclear weapons, fighting terrorism, and so on) limit the sphere of the confrontation and, therefore, its nature.

Others see it quite differently: For them the Ukrainian crisis is the firebox of an all-encompassing animosity. Every aspect of the relationship, every interaction, every issue has been or will be contaminated by the ill intentions each attributes to the other. The hostility they now bear toward each other and the deep suspicion each has of the other's aims infect nearly all dimensions, from nuclear arms to energy relations, from threats to European security to regional conflicts. Even on issues where they are still cooperating, such as Iran's nuclear program or the nuclear non-proliferation regime, the poison is likely to seep in. Had the Iranian agreement, for example, not been achieved in July 2015, Russia almost certainly would not have joined in a new round of intensified sanctions. Moreover, were the Ukrainian crisis to end tomorrow, the damage has been done and its effects will be ongoing.

A second perspective on the Cold War provides a different angle on today's US–Russian confrontation. "Was the Cold War a security dilemma?," Robert Jervis once asked (Jervis, 2001). It is a perversity of international politics that a state, in fashioning security for itself, leaves other states unsure whether their own security thereby may not be endangered, leading them to beef up their own security efforts, thus ratcheting up the response of the first state. The dilemma arises from the fact that, even if neither means harm to the other, neither, in any other than a friendly relationship, can be sure of that. It deepens when defensive motives by either or both are pursued by offensive means. Then muddy waters leave uncertain whether the security dilemma is simply irrelevant and the problem is a state bent on aggression with no security goal in mind.

That, many in the West think, applies to the current situation. Russian aggression in Ukraine, they are convinced, was foretold by Putin's earlier reference to the collapse of the Soviet Union as "the greatest geopolitical catastrophe of the century" (Putin, 2005). A decade later, they would argue, he set about reversing this outcome, not in defense of Russian security, but to reassemble as many pieces of the former empire as he could.[1]

If, however, the new US–Russian Cold War is some version of the security dilemma, the complexities are different. For example, intentions, even if benign or driven by defensive concerns, are difficult to judge. Actions speak louder, and, when they are or appear aggressive, they naturally resolve ambiguity by promoting suspicion and a move to man the ramparts. Even if a state assumes the best about another state and wishes to assure it of its own peaceful intentions, if there is no reassuring the other side, the dilemma deepens. Stalin, because of a worldview that regarded capitalist states as implacably hostile, may have been incapable of being reassured. If so, then, even if the Cold War was a security dilemma, at best it was what Jervis calls a "deep security dilemma."

Perhaps the same is true today. That is, conceivably Putin and those around him have not only convinced themselves that the Obama administration means to ring Russia with a bulwark of anti-Russian neighbors and, worse, to sabotage the Russian regime from within, but also see this agenda as in the nature of fundamental forces shaping US foreign policy before, during, and after this administration. On the US side, elements making for a deep security dilemma may also exist. The administration may, indeed, be innocent of the malevolence Moscow sees in its policy *but* be aware that this is the perception of Putin and those around him, yet persuaded that they are incorrigible, and nothing the United States can do will change their mind.

Conceiving the Cold War as a security dilemma – deep or otherwise – underscores how much more intense it makes the unhappy reality that, under its influence, as Jervis (2001) notes, "the interaction between states *generates* strife rather than merely revealing or accentuating conflicts stemming from differences over goals." Because of it, "international politics can be seen as tragic in the sense that states may desire – or at least be willing to settle for – mutual security, but their own behavior puts this very goal further from their reach." The new Russia–West Cold War both dramatizes the point and signals how obstacle-strewn the path out will be.

Assessing the Cold War

In the end, the most fundamental questions about the Cold War are all "why" questions? Why did it happen? Why did it take the form that it did? Why did it last as long as it did? Why did it end? And why did it end when it did? Answering the first question is easiest. The likelihood that two powers standing alone amid the vast wreckage of World War II, the embodiment of antithetical political and economic systems, each persuaded the other represented some version of the threat that it had just fought a war to defeat, each driven to assert itself farther afield than ever before would lead to a charged rivalry was, if not inevitable, the next closest thing. The more challenging question is why this rivalry took the form that it did. Why so deep, so militarized, so universal, so uncompromising?

The facile answer at the time, and one to which some scholars have returned, is Stalin: his narcissistic paranoia and pathologically entangled Marxist-Leninist view of the world coupled with his outsized imperial impulse guaranteed that a predicable competition would take on the deeper and darker tones that it did. For others the picture is more complicated. Stalin's paranoia, the alien character of the system over which he presided, and his aggressive moves in the war's wake stimulated an understandably hostile reaction from European states, ravaged and prostrate, and from the United States, fearful of standing alone should Europe succumb to chaos or Soviet diktat.

In fact, however, the historical evidence now indicates that Stalin and those around him did genuinely fear a revitalized German threat (and the same from Japan), made more ominous by the West's readiness to partner with them in developing a policy increasingly directed against the Soviet Union. Amid the rubble opportunities beckoned – opportunities that Stalin was all too eager to seize – but, at the same time, some of his most aggressive actions had more to do with what he imagined to be the United States' menacing intentions. In the haze of a world still smoldering from war, without anchors or safeguards, and teeming with uncertainties, it was natural that East and West would act on their worst assumptions. These led both sides to accent the prospect of war and to ready themselves for it. The early and intense militarization of the fledgling competition produced a spiral of suspicion and hostile moves that, like a ratchet, locked the relationship into an ever tightening cold war.

Their inflated responses, while entirely understandable at the time, do not change the basic reality – leaders on both sides got it wrong. Each misread the threat posed by the other, and, when they acted on their misreading, they produced a denser and more intractable confrontation than was necessary. In this there is a lesson. Yielding too quickly to the gravest assessment of threat may appear prudent, but it also has costs. In this case, not only were these a hardening of the Cold War but, potentially, the loss of a historically better outcome in Europe. George Kennan, the author of the containment doctrine, from the start insisted that the Soviet Union had no intention of rolling its tanks into Western Europe. The threat it posed was political, a threat accentuated by these countries' vulnerability to Soviet subversion because of their economic frailty and political instability – a threat requiring a political and economic response, not a military one. As he later described his frustration when in 1948 he watched the growing momentum leading to the creation of NATO: "Why did they [the proponents of a military alliance] wish to divert attention from a thoroughly justified and promising program of economic recovery by emphasizing a danger which did not actually exist but which might indeed be brought into existence by too much discussion of the military balance and by the ostentatious stimulation of a military rivalry?" (Kennan, 1972).

Framing the relationship as a military contest, Kennan was convinced, would split Europe into two blocs and entrench the Soviet Union in one of them. In fall 1948, at the height of a crisis over Berlin manufactured by Stalin's power move to cut off the West's access to their sectors of the occupied city, Kennan, then head of the State Department's Policy Planning Staff, proposed withdrawing all occupying forces from Germany and reunifying the country under a freely elected provisional government. Stalin, he knew, would initially refuse, but he calculated that the vision of a unified, neutral Germany at the heart of a reintegrated Europe, acting as an independent "third force" in international politics, would eventually acquire its own momentum. In Washington the idea fell flat, first, because some abhorred the idea of Europe as a third force with a reunified Germany at its core, but more because the overriding priority had become creating a West German entity integrated into an economically refurbished Western Europe.[2]

As for the Soviet side of the story, it turned out that Kennan's "Plan A" was not as madcap as many assumed. Even after the formal creation of the Federal Republic of Germany, Stalin had apparently harbored the illusion that a reunified Germany might well tilt in the Soviet direction, and as late as 1952 he offered his own plan for a reunified and neutralized Germany. Western leaders treated it as merely a ploy to disrupt plans to integrate West Germany into a West European defense community, which it may well have been. But, if that was its objective, they might have tested the price the Soviets were willing to pay to achieve it. This they did not do for the same two reasons they gave Kennan's Plan A no hearing.

There are a number of ways to think about the reason that the Cold War lasted as long as it did. Surely one explanation resides in the nature of the hegemons that presided over the contest and the diametrically opposed notions that generation after generation of their leaders and political elite had of history, the forces driving contemporary international politics, and the impulses behind the other side's policies. In addition, the depth, passion, and scale that the Cold War acquired between the Berlin blockade in 1948 and the Korean War in 1950 gave the standoff an impulse that carried it decades forward, and the cycle of violence, from Southeast Asia to the Middle East, from Africa to Central America, provided never ending occasion to exploit or fear the role of the other side in it. Then, too, once an arms competition gathers steam, as it did coming out of the Korean War, it takes on a self-perpetuating momentum that reinforces underlying hostile attitudes. But perhaps the most dramatic reason for the Cold War's length was in what did not happen: war or revolution would have abruptly ended it, either by destroying or by transforming one or both sides. What John Lewis Gaddis called the "long peace," by which he meant not the absence of war during the Cold War but no war between the United States and the Soviet Union, may have been due to the sobering impact of nuclear weapons, as many believe, or to the shadow cast by World War II. Whichever it was, or both, as a result, nothing intervened to cut short the powerful inertia of the rivalry.

Almost certainly, however, the Cold War would have arrived at an abrupt denouement much sooner but for one further factor: the change it underwent in subsequent decades. Gradually, if erratically and unsteadily, the Cold War evolved, shedding its most dangerous features and taking on something resembling rules of restraint – some of them formally negotiated, others unacknowledged but real. Indeed, scarcely had Stalin been interred in the Kremlin Wall and the Korean War called off, than the two sides began signaling an interest in releasing themselves from the sterile, frozen deadlock they were in. The new Soviet leadership softened its stance at the United Nations, reached out to India, Turkey, and Yugoslavia, and moderated its tone toward the United States. When President Eisenhower met with them at the Geneva summit in July 1955 they talked about nuclear disarmament and European security, albeit not in terms promising success, and Eisenhower tried out his equally dead-end "Open-Skies" proposal, a plan intended to constrain a nuclear arms buildup. Still, it was a start – the first step toward substituting what Adam Ulam called "imprecise friendliness" for the icy hostility of a few years earlier (Ulam, 1974, p. 569). A year later, at the famous Party congress where he denounced Stalin, Nikita Khrushchev introduced the concept of "peaceful coexistence" (or, rather, resuscitated it, since it had an earlier life in the first years after the 1917 Bolshevik revolution). Nuclear weapons had rendered a part of the Soviet canon treating "war as inevitable" as long as capitalism survived a dangerous anachronism.

None of this – or, for that matter, further change to come – guaranteed that the Cold War would not lurch into deep crisis. Indeed, two years after Khrushchev's ideological volte-face, the Soviet Union launched the first of a series of confrontations over Berlin, culminating in the October 1962 Cuban missile crisis, moments as dangerous as any during the Cold War. A decade later, during the October 1973 "Yom Kippur War" in the Middle East, the specter of nuclear war again loomed. And one decade after that, in the first years of the Reagan administration, the two sides slid back into deep Cold War, with nuclear war once more at the forefront of people's minds.

Yet, each of these ominous interludes either preceded or introduced marked change in the Cold War. In the wake of the four-year crisis over Berlin and then Cuba, the two countries swiftly agreed to the 1963 nuclear test ban treaty and by the end of the decade began negotiating limitations on what until then had been an open-ended nuclear arms race. The 1973 Arab-Israeli War occurred in the middle of the early 1970s US-Soviet détente and, for all its drama, attested to the change this phase of the Cold War had brought. Although the United States had gone to a DEFCON 3 alert at a critical stage of the war (its highest war alert ever was DEFCON 2 during the Cuban missile crisis), Henry Kissinger had also flown to Moscow with what turned out to be a justified expectation that the two countries could cooperate in containing the war's escalation.

The period of détente itself represented an important, although largely misunderstood stage in the Cold War. It both altered the character of the confrontation and fell victim to what in that confrontation the two governments failed to alter. The Nixon administration, struggling with the limits of its power exposed by the Vietnam War and the implications of an ongoing rivalry with a nuclear power that was now its rough equal, embraced détente as a more sustainable form of containment. For Leonid Brezhnev and his colleagues, détente constituted recognition as a player of equal weight to the United States – equal in the security to which it was entitled, equal in determining the direction of the US-Soviet military competition, and equal in dealing with the world's trouble spots. As Andrei Gromyko, the Soviet foreign minister, expressed it, "No major international problem is being settled or can be settled today without Soviet participation."[3]

Had the assumptions each side brought to détente held, the tenor and nature of the Cold War would have changed fundamentally. But they did not. On the one side, the Nixon administration had no intention of treating Russia as an equal. On the contrary, détente for it applied to select areas of the relationship and was not intended to allow Moscow to interfere with its diplomacy in the Middle East or its war in Southeast Asia. Moreover, Nixon and his secretary of state counted on the United States' new opening with China to give them the upper hand in dealings with the Soviet Union. On the other side, Soviet leaders never meant to bind their hands in aiding where possible revolutionary change in the Third World. The lesson here is not that détente as a concept was fraudulent – as many of its critics insisted – but that it was too narrowly framed. By confining it to nuclear arms control with a dollop of economic cooperation, it left out the sphere most likely to destroy the whole undertaking. Whether the two governments could have agreed to constructive limits on their role in the world's most unstable regions is uncertain; what is certain is that, by not trying, they guaranteed détente's failure.

As the new US–Russia Cold War moves through stages – as it surely will – when the two sides relent and seek their own détente, the earlier experience will have an echo in two respects: first, contemporary Russia's preoccupation with being treated as an equal resonates no less powerfully than it did for Brezhnev's Soviet Union. Second, success will depend on mutually acceptable rules of the game where, from the beginning, the interaction between the United States and Russia has been the most fraught – in this case, the countries that once comprised the Soviet Union.

Before the Cold War's final chapter was written, a third period of tension and rancor intervened. During Ronald Reagan's first term, from 1981 to 1984, the combined effect of the ongoing war in Afghanistan, Soviet support for the Sandinista insurgency in Central America, and the administration's determination to reverse what it saw as a loss of military advantage to the Soviet Union reignited the Cold War and sent the two sides stumbling unsteadily in unknown directions. It turned out to be the penultimate stage in the Cold War and something of an exclamation point to it, underscoring the bankruptcy of the Soviet order and the folly, or by now maybe simply the irrelevance, of a contest that, for all the change undergone, had lasted too long.

What matters most when thinking about this history in the context of the moment, however, is that the original Cold War did not remain the same. It passed through stages and, as a result, while never until the very end transcending its basic character as a US–Soviet rivalry, moved far beyond its primitive, unyielding early phase. Over time the five characteristics that, as suggested in chapter 1, distinguished the Cold War at its height gradually weakened, even in some cases fading entirely. If the new US–Russia Cold War has any chance of being as short and shallow as possible – the goal that I am arguing should be at the center of both countries' current foreign policy – that will depend on how soon a parallel process begins and how compressed its stages are. This, in turn, will depend on how soon and how intensely leadership on both sides shifts gears and together makes this its priority.

In the original Cold War, the first quality to give way was the notion that engaging the other side served no purpose. After some dithering, first on the US side, then on the Soviet side, the Big Four (France, the UK, the Soviet Union, and the United States) agreed to have their foreign ministers meet in Berlin in January 1954 to discuss the German question and the unresolved status of an occupied Austria. In summer 1955 the four heads of state met in Geneva for the first summit since three of them had convened in Potsdam ten years earlier, before there was a Cold War. In 1959, after another Big Four foreign ministers' conference, and despite the Soviet intervention in Hungary and the Suez

War in 1956, the Soviet ultimatum over Berlin in 1958, and a Chinese-inspired crisis in the Formosa Straits that same year, Khrushchev arrived in the United States, still ostensibly looking for a diplomatic way forward.

At this stage of the Cold War, the most that could be said is that the two sides had dropped their unwillingness to talk and reintroduced diplomacy into the relationship, not that they were yet willing to propose steps on which they could agree. That was the next stage. In 1963, sobered by near catastrophe in the Cuban missile crisis, Moscow and Washington took seriously the need to find common ground and, by what was a record time in arms control negotiations, agreed to ban nuclear testing other than underground. Khrushchev's earlier proposals for "general and complete disarmament," and even the somewhat more serious 1957 Rapacki Plan to create a nuclear-free zone in Central Europe, had done little to shake another feature of the early Cold War: the assumption that the cross-purposes embodied in the two systems made accommodation impossible or, where not, undesirable. The comprehensive test ban treaty, followed by the 1967 nuclear non-proliferation treaty and, beginning in 1969, progress toward a strategic nuclear arms accord, proved to the two that, fundamental differences notwithstanding, they could reach mutually beneficial agreements.

Then in the 1970s came the most significant transformation of the Cold War's original essence. To the extent that the détente that Nixon and Brezhnev pursued implied a readiness to manage rather than fight the Cold War, they were acknowledging that, however they distributed major blame, the problem lay in the interaction of the two sides, not simply in the nature and behavior of one side only. In practical form, it was the culmination of a shifting attitude tracing back to John Kennedy's eloquent 1963 commencement address at American

University: "I have," he began, "therefore, chosen this time and this place to discuss a topic on which ignorance too often abounds and the truth is too rarely perceived – yet it is the most important topic on earth: world peace." The olive branch that he extended to the Soviet side stressed the two countries' deeply painful experience with war. "No nation in the history of battle," he said, "ever suffered more than the Soviet Union suffered in the course of the Second World War." But, he continued, much as "our two countries" are bound by "our mutual abhorrence of war," we are "both caught up in a vicious and dangerous cycle in which suspicion on one side breeds suspicion on the other, and new weapons beget counter-weapons." And then he said,

> Let us reexamine our attitude toward the cold war, remembering that we are not engaged in a debate seeking to pile up debating points. We are not here distributing blame or pointing the finger of judgment. We must deal with the world as it is, and not as it might have been had the history of the last 18 years been different.

Not only, however, did the brief interlude of détente constitute the point at which both sides had most plainly ceased believing that the "essence of the problem was in the essence of the other side," conceding that a contest renounced by neither could be kept within safer and more constructive limits only if each approached it as a matter of mutual responsibility. They also set aside a fourth defining characteristic of the original Cold War – the conviction that any agreement with the other side could only be tactical and one-off. Instead, as Kissinger explained when announcing the new Strategic Arms Limitation Treaty (SALT) in June 1972: "We have ... sought to move forward across a broad range of issues so that progress in one area would add momentum to the progress of other areas." Both now counted on the cumulative effect from a widening weave of agreements as a better means to alter the other side's behavior. Détente was to be a collaboration of sorts by which the other's worst inclinations were best disciplined.

What had not changed throughout the Cold War's evolution, however, was the unquestioned assumption that the competition between the United States and the Soviet Union could only be moderated, not eliminated – not as long as by their basic nature the two contestants remained fundamentally different. Ending the Cold War, therefore, was neither the logical next step nor the inevitable consequence of irresistible historical forces. And, thus, answering the questions why it ended, why it ended when it did, and why it ended as it did presents no small challenge.

How one answers the first question depends on one's answer to the second question. Those who believe that the Cold War ended only with the demise of the Soviet Union will go looking for their explanation in the reason(s) the Soviet Union collapsed. As an explanation its logical contemporary parallel would be that the new US–Russian Cold War will end, not with leadership change or a change in Russian behavior, but only when the political system currently in place gives way to another. Those, however, who believe the Cold War ended sooner – and they are most of the scholars studying this period – locate the explanation elsewhere. Precisely where depends on the criteria used for calling it over. If the criterion is when the end assumed concrete form, then many would favor 1990 and German reunification.

An arguably more meaningful measure is at what point the two sides regarded the Cold War as over. That happened, say a number of observers, when Bush met Gorbachev in Malta in December 1989 for the "seasick summit," held on US and Soviet ships amid hurricane-whipped waves into which the US president nearly plunged when struggling to board one of the ships. That, of course, would have been noteworthy, but still more so was what transpired between the two men. At one point in the meeting Gorbachev turned to Bush and said, "We want you in Europe, you need to be in Europe. It's important for the future of Europe that you are in Europe. . . . We don't consider you an enemy anymore. Things have changed. We don't think of you in those terms" (Wohlforth, 2003, p. 43). It was not a spur-of-the-moment remark. Anatoly Chernyaev, Gorbachev's principal foreign policy advisor, said in March 1996, at a Princeton University conference where this moment was recalled, that the Soviet leader had been thinking in these terms months before the meeting.

Bush, in turn, went out of his way to stress his administration's desire to assist Gorbachev's reform efforts and to engage the constructive US–Soviet agenda Gorbachev was urging. He recounted how, on his way to the summit, he changed his perspective on the stake the United States had in Gorbachev's success "by 180 degrees" (Service, 2015, p. 421). While this referred more to his initial skepticism about the wisdom of investing too heavily in the prospect of real change in the Soviet Union than to a cold war epiphany, the Soviet side treated the administration's readiness to help as stunning proof that the contest was over.

In the end, while it took two to produce a cold war, only one was needed to end it. The revolution that Gorbachev worked in Soviet foreign and defense policy between 1986 and 1987 sucked the air out of the Cold War. Disagreements over the issues of the day continued until the very end – and these were, indeed, dramatic, including German reunification, the collapse of socialism in Eastern Europe, and the Soviet war in Afghanistan. But both sides now approached the discord much as any two countries approach matters on which they disagree, not as the Cold War's next installment.

Rarely has a leader so swiftly and thoroughly transformed the foreign policy of his country as Gorbachev did during these two years. Others have described in detail the sweep of his innovations, but they literally tore up root and branch the long-standing, albeit increasingly prostituted ideological principles underlying Soviet foreign policy, the distended agenda generations of Soviet leaders had pursued, as well as Soviet military doctrine and the core of defense planning (Brown, 2012; Zubok, 2003; English, 2003, 2000; Garthoff, 2015). By the end of 1986, he had introduced a new military doctrine reversing the role of Soviet armed forces in war and peace, planned their considerable downsizing, and, after the Chernobyl nuclear reactor disaster, put the reduction and eventual elimination of nuclear weapons at the top of his agenda. He was already far along in jettisoning the shopworn notions of "class struggle" and international politics as the clash of two social systems, and advancing in their place the proposition that world order mattered more than prevailing in competitive relationships. If the large challenges that stood in the way of greater common welfare and security were to be addressed, he and those closest to him decided that it could only be in partnership with the West.

This radically altered approach was not the product of a coherent vision that emerged whole, its parts neatly integrated. On the contrary, it reflected the force of impulse, partly the product of Gorbachev's personality, partly a slowly congealing sense as he and his colleagues struggled with the mess that they had inherited from their decrepit predecessors, much of it the unanticipated but logical follow-on to what they launched. The revolution in thinking to which it gave rise, however, was powerful – so powerful that Gorbachev set about acting on it before he had any clear evidence that the United States was aboard. All of it, alas, constitutes an inauspicious parallel for the Russia–West Cold War of our day, for there is no Gorbachev on either side and no indication that one awaits beyond the next series of presidential elections.

Still, there are lessons in the story of the Cold War's end worth reflecting on. There may be little chance of a Gorbachev-like breakthrough any time soon, but the larger contextual features that allowed or, some would say, induced his foreign policy revolution may be relevant. Had the Soviet Union not been in the disrepair that it was as the last of the Brezhnev-era relics left the scene, it is difficult to imagine that Gorbachev – even assuming that he had made it to the top – would have felt the need to strike out as boldly as he did. Translated closer to our day, should Russia remain stalled between a reform dead in the water and priorities that leave modernization of the country on a back burner, at some point its decline may create pressure to rethink how it wants to play its hand and with whom – even sooner if the economic strains under which the Russian economy currently labors deepen and then burgeon into a full-blown political-economic crisis.

Were Russia, under this or a different leadership, to provide even faint signs of wishing to explore a shift in course, two lessons from this earlier period are worth weighing. The first is that the inertia of preconceptions jeopardizes opportunity. Both the Reagan and Bush administrations were slow to recognize the significance of the changes Gorbachev was making, because their fixed notions about Soviet leaders ensured that their first reaction would be skepticism and caution. Even though, by early 1984, Reagan had begun to move beyond the hard line of his first years in office, it took him two years into Gorbachev's tenure to realize that he had a willing partner. Some of the delay was due to the influence of those in the administration deeply persuaded that Gorbachev was more of the same, only cleverer, but the effect was to postpone the start of a fundamentally new US–Soviet relationship and to make life more difficult for Gorbachev back home. When Bush arrived in office in 1989, he imposed a new six-month delay to carry out a basic policy review, inspired in no small part by the conviction among senior members of his administration that Reagan had by the end allowed himself to be too taken with the Soviet leader. Again, the process was waylaid. In the end, both delays limited how far and deep the transformation of international relations that Gorbachev sought could go in what turned out to be his limited time in office.

In more specific ways, the reflexive skepticism that governed US responses to Gorbachev's bold ideas carried over to narrower but important missed opportunities. For example, one of the issues that has complicated the post-Cold War arms control process has been the unwillingness of the Russians to negotiate any limits on the large store of tactical nuclear weapons still in the Russian arsenal. At the July 1991 Moscow summit between Bush and Gorbachev, the Soviet side sought to set a date to start negotiations on reducing tactical nuclear weapons in Europe. The US side, old habits of thought still intact, refused (Garthoff, 1994).[4]

The other lesson is more positive, but, by all indications, one that will have to be relearned. Gorbachev may have been the driving force behind the change promoting the end of the Cold War, but along the way Reagan contributed his own part – no portion of which was more important than the basic principle that he insisted should guide US conduct. When addressing the Soviet side, as Jack Matlock, his senior advisor and later ambassador to the Soviet Union, recalled, issues were to be framed not in terms of "you gotta do this or you gotta do that," but "how do we find common ground allowing us to cooperate in ways serving each side's interests?" (Matlock, 2015). In writing about this period, Matlock added his own piece of advice to later US (and Russian) policymakers: "They might also turn some attention to

Gorbachev's adage (to which Reagan would have agreed heartily) that no country can ensure its own security without regarding the security of others" (Matlock, 2004).

The Cold War's Legacy

When the Cold War ended, it did not release its hold on history. On the contrary, like the Ancient Mariner's albatross, it continued to haunt US and Russian efforts to build a new relationship every step of the way. It was not supposed to be that way. Leaders on both sides thought that they had closed that book, and they congratulated themselves on how skillfully they had written its last chapter.

In truth, however, stunning as was the peaceful reunification of Germany and the comparatively bloodless collapse of the Soviet empire, the thick residue of mistrust and unreconstructed thinking, accumulated over a half century of Cold War, remained in place. Each side assumed, without much second thought, that, as they dismantled the struts and buttresses of the Cold War, associated attitudes would perish with them. In this spirit, Gorbachev and his foreign minister, in particular, went out of their way to expunge the notion of the two sides as adversaries. What they called the "enemy image" no longer belonged, they insisted, and should be discarded. Initially they directed their admonition at the United States, frustrated by what they viewed as a tardy US recognition of the transformation taking place in Russian foreign policy. As the pace of change quickened, Georgy Arbatov, the prominent director of the USA and Canada Institute of the Soviet (now Russian) Academy of Sciences, would tease his American audiences by saying, "We are going to do the cruelest thing to you. We are going to deny you the enemy image you so like."[5] Soon, however, they included themselves. They too had a distorted impression of US aspirations and intentions. They too had delayed an earlier end to the Cold War by clinging to hoary stereotypes. While changing Washington's attitude toward the Soviet Union remained crucial, a first deputy foreign minister, Anatoly Kovalev, reminded his colleagues in the ministry that "we ourselves have so far done little to demolish the analogous stereotype in the consciousness of the Soviet people. One without the other will hardly work" (Garthoff, 2015, p. 82).

Only the surface malignancy, however, had been removed. It mattered, of course, that Gorbachev had stopped thinking of the United States as an adversary and that, in the early years after the collapse of the Soviet Union, when US leaders and their new Russian counterparts came together, threat analysis was far from their minds. Indeed, when reflecting on the last years of the Cold War, those who were present later laid heavy stress on the importance of growing trust between leaders, even on the importance of consciously striving to build trust by taking responsibility for one's own actions. At the 1996 Princeton conference, Chernyaev commented that "from the start Gorbachev trusted Bush and Baker in the sense that he never doubted their sincerity, he never put their words in question" (Wohlforth, 2003, p. 35). From the Malta summit, he said, "I have notes that were taken during the discussions between Gorbachev and Bush and Gorbachev and Baker that really prove that there was a human rapport among them, that Gorbachev actually in a personal way trusted those people. And it was my impression that they reciprocated." Baker instantly interjected, "Well, I can confirm that we did."

Even more striking, by 1986 Gorbachev had come to realize that trust could not be built unless his side recognized and then addressed the sources of the other side's mistrust. His conversations with Margaret Thatcher, in particular, had been frank and, for him, revealing. She bluntly told him, "You have no democracy, so there's no control over the government. It does what it wants . . . Let's say we trust you personally, but if you're gone tomorrow then what?" (English, 2003, pp. 265–6). As he reported to the Politburo: "She focused on trust. She said, 'the USSR has squandered the West's faith and we don't trust you. You take grave actions lightly: Hungary, Czechoslovakia, Afghanistan . . . We're afraid of you.'" After including more of her indictment, he concluded: "That's how she sees it. She thinks we haven't rejected the 'Brezhnev Doctrine.' Comrades, we have to think this over. We can't ignore these arguments." Add this to the list of lessons from the Cold War. Had at least one side to the conflict not been willing to take a hard look at its own behavior and weigh its impact on the other side, it is difficult to imagine how the cycle of mistrust could have been broken, even if one or both sides wanted to break it. In the new Cold War, until one or both sides follow Gorbachev's example, neither is the current cycle of mistrust likely to be broken.

Trust between leaders, however, turns out not to be the same as trust between countries. The change that occurred at the leadership level was critical in terminating the Cold War and in shaping its end. But it was not sufficient to guarantee a sequel that met the hopes and expectations of those who followed. How far it fell short is addressed in chapter 3. However, it is fair to say that, despite the soaring rhetoric and casual optimism in the first two or three years of the post-Cold War era, almost from the start the hopes each side had for the other were damaged by the unexpected turns that politics took. Each soon found reason to protest the actions of the other, and all along the way the legacy of the Cold War laid its dead hand on the controversies and discontents that began to surface. But leaders did not have their minds on the weight of the past. Beguiled by the new world unfolding before them, and trusting the reworked mindsets of the people with whom they dealt, they spent little time contemplating the rusted hulk of the Cold War. It, however, had never been to do simply with the leaders who conducted it. The Cold War was a sprawling, massive political and organizational affair, and most of this remained in place.

The Warsaw Treaty Organization, the Soviet Union's alliance system, had disintegrated, but NATO stood as it always had, with a new Strategic Concept (1991), followed by reduced force levels and a modified operational doctrine, but nonetheless with its fundamental structure, ramified institutions, and basic capabilities intact. The Coordinating Committee for Multilateral Export Controls (COCOM), the allied mechanism for blocking the sale of arms and related technologies to the Soviet Union and its allies, continued in force until 1994 and its provisions until 1996. The Jackson–Vanik Amendment that denied the Soviet Union most-favored-nation trading status because of Soviet restrictions on Jewish immigration, although waived annually in Russia's case, was not repealed until 2012.

On the other side, the bloated Soviet military was in shambles, military units decomposing, military command demoralized, arms and equipment unmaintained and rusting, but at the same time little in its structure, doctrine, and modus operandi had changed. If failure is the metric, scarcely any other policy realm in the new Russia met it more regularly and thoroughly than the repeated false starts with military reform. Rather than adjusting to meet new security threats, as Alexei Arbatov, one of Russia's ablest military analysts, reported, "It would not be an exaggeration to say that Russia's armed forces – with a troop strength projected to be more than 1 million by 2004 – are 70–80 percent oriented toward a war with the West (as well as Turkey and Japan)" (Arbatov, 2004, p. 106). To be more precise, he wrote, "At least 90 percent of Russia's strategic and tactical nuclear forces and its command and control and early warning complex, three largest military districts out of six, and three of the four fleets are aimed at war against the West." In the 1990s, Russia's intelligence services, the successors to the Soviet KGB, underwent various organizational tweaks, with foreign intelligence spun off as an independent agency (the SVR) and the Border Troops initially set apart. But they too retained much of their former institutional identity and outlook.

How much of the Cold War edifice survived, however, mattered less than the durability of mentalities that had sustained it. NATO, as its 1991 Strategic Concept proclaimed, may have concluded that the "threat of a simultaneous, full-scale attack on all of NATO's European fronts has effectively been removed and thus no longer provides the focus for Allied strategy," but the threat that portions of the Russian political elite and much of the military saw in NATO lingered largely unchanged. Russian leaders could profess, as often as they liked, that Russia was without enemies, and even write their claim into official military doctrine, but the dense encrustation of mistrust that permeated large segments of Russian society – the many agencies and political figures who had never bought into Gorbachev's foreign policy revolution – remained just below the surface. Slowly, steadily, it fed its poison into the politics surrounding Russia's increasingly frequent disagreements with NATO (none angrier than over NATO enlargement) and at a deeper level into the growing opposition to many aspects of US policy.

Deep suspicions, enriched with wild conspiracy theories, had thrived in many quarters in the fading moments of the Cold War, and these came through the collapse unscathed, eventually spreading, in only mildly attenuated form, to a wider portion of the political class. Alexander Prokhanov is a right-wing primal Russian nationalist, successful novelist and newspaper editor. In a 1992 interview, he lashed out at the *New Yorker*'s David Remnick: "You did it! . . . The general concept was yours – the CIA's. I am sure of it" (Remnick, 1992). His rant was over the collapse of the Soviet Union, and it went: "The process was regulated and designed by your people . . . Do you think East Germany fell apart on its own? Do you think Poland, Bulgaria, Yugoslavia, and, finally, the Soviet Union fell apart on their own?" For this occasion he directed his rage against the United States and its "tool," Mikhail Gorbachev, but his real target at the time was Boris Yeltsin for gullibly collaborating with an ill-intentioned United States. In this he had many allies, including Gennady Zuganov, the head of the Communist Party, Russia's second largest political party, who, when Yeltsin's government, having lost the struggle to block NATO enlargement, weakly agreed to a charter of its own with NATO, called it treason. He had already compared the Partnership for Peace, the cooperative framework that NATO had worked out for non-NATO members and that Russia had joined in 1994, to Operation Barbarossa, the plan that guided Hitler's invasion of the Soviet Union in 1941. During these years the hypertrophied level of mistrust that Prokhanov, Zuganov, and a sizable number of ex-Soviet generals, prominent cultural figures, and politicians exhibited never reached critical mass, but it was part of an atmosphere with which leadership had to contend. Gradually, as that atmosphere evolved, it merged into the mainstream. In the new US–Russia Cold War, Prokhanov still froths as before, but no longer from the outside; he is now a steady and celebrated presence on Russian television and in the press.

In the United States the mistrust generated by the Cold War, at least initially, appeared to dissipate, although, among the neo-conservatives and the more hawkish of the cold warriors, Russia quickly resumed its place as a trouble-maker and threat. Thus, by 1994, the columnist Charles Krauthammer had satisfied himself that "the debate about how to deal with Russia really comes to an end" (Krauthammer, 1994).

Russia's invasion of Chechnya, on top of the trouble it had stirred up elsewhere, had settled it. Before, "one school viewed Russia as incorrigibly expansionist and in need of restraining by the West. The other school held that so long as the evolution of Russia along democratic capitalist lines proceeded, we should do nothing that might jeopardize that evolution." The "events of 1994," he wrote, "have made the second view moot." Hardliners from the Reagan administration, such as Casper Weinberger, when he warned that Russia was maneuvering to cut the United States out of the Central Asian energy market, had reached pretty much the same conclusion (Weinberger and Schweizer, 1997).

Krauthammer, however, was wrong. Most people, including within the Clinton administration, had not decided that Yeltsin's Russia was "incorrigibly expansionist" and "in need of restraining." Yet, while the jaundice that animated those who found it difficult to think of Russia in terms different from the Soviet Union had little echo within the administration of either Bush senior or Clinton, mistrust – or the potential for it – was not absent. It lingered, at a minimum, at the subconscious level. For example, when in 1991 senior figures in the Bush administration, such as Secretary of State James Baker, urgently sought to withdraw Soviet nuclear weapons from Ukraine, Belarus, and Kazakhstan and ensure central control over them, others, such as National Security Advisor Brent Scowcroft, were not so sure that it might not be okay to leave them where they were as a check on a future less peaceful Russia.[6] Well into the post-Soviet period, senior defense officials, while scarcely suggesting that Russia was or would soon be a security threat, nonetheless had in the back of their mind that, in a decade or more, "the potential for Russia to re-emerge as a large and capable regional military rival of the United States increases significantly" (Hughes, 1997). The mistrust that percolated either at a boil or as an unarticulated prudent hedge through the 1990s gnawed at the relationship and complicated the way moments of tension were handled. But, as on the Russian side, its more baneful effect came in the new US–Russia Cold War, when its full-bodied version triumphed.

Mistrust, however, has been a far more pernicious part of the Cold War's legacy than simply the damage done directly. Its indirect role has badly twisted and warped the context within which the United States and Russia struggle to manage their relationship. It is a scourge rooted in the origins of the Cold War and in a good deal of history before. For nothing has plagued Russia's efforts to place its relations with Europe and the United States on a modern, constructive footing more than the deep hostility and suspicion that those countries once under its rule maintain toward it. The Norwegian historian Geir Lundestad once described the post-World War II community over which the United States presided as "an empire by invitation." The Soviet empire was anything but, and the means by which it subjected and then controlled neighboring countries guaranteed that, when it passed, its legacy would be toxic. The end of the Cold War, therefore, had different meanings in the West from those in former dominions. For Poles, Hungarians, and other Eastern Europeans it did mean freedom and independence, but not, as for the West – at least not in their minds – a safer world beyond their borders. On the contrary, the threat that the West saw in the Soviet Union was transferred to its Russian successor. As a result, they wanted not only to shelter within the West's security institutions but for those institutions to deal with the Russian threat as they had the Soviet one. And, in turn, the Russians saw these governments not only as unfriendly but as a retrograde influence within the institutions the United States and its old allies hoped would either be acceptable to Russia (such as NATO and the European Union) or as venues for cooperation (such as the Organization for Security and Cooperation in Europe [OSCE] and the Council of Europe).

Perhaps it was too much to expect a country buried in the debris of a collapsing empire to rise above its history and set about building a relationship with its former Warsaw Pact allies inspiring trust and good will, but the insouciance with which the Russians avoided the past had a hefty price. When the nucleus of that empire finally splintered and the Soviet Union's parts became independent countries, Russian leaders found it still more difficult to substitute for coercion and the heavy hand an approach featuring methods and goals designed to reassure. Mistrust already built in, therefore, rather than being reduced, was through mutual action-reaction constantly reinforced. Mistrust at both levels – the residue of the US–Soviet Cold War and the residue of colonial history – flowed together and together formed the dark and damaging substrata impeding and ultimately wrecking US and Russian efforts to put the Cold War far behind and construct a fundamentally different relationship. How the two countries stumbled toward and then into a new Cold War, however, is a separate and crucial issue, and exploring that is what comes next.

3

The Descent

They were like two old friends at a college reunion admiring the other's career. "I'm just tremendously impressed by his wisdom," Boris Yeltsin gushed. "I think he has incredible qualities not only as a political person but also as a person, as a really great political figure of the United States" (Wines, 1992). In turn George H. W. Bush said of Yeltsin, "[I have] a very warm feeling in my heart about what he has done and is trying to do, and I consider him my friend." It was February 1992, and Yeltsin was winding up his first visit to the United States as president of a newly independent Russia. Earlier in the day the two men had signed a declaration announcing that "Russia and the United States do not regard each other as potential adversaries. From now on, the relationship will be characterized by friendship and partnership founded on mutual trust and respect and a common commitment to democracy and economic freedom." "In the future," Yeltsin boasted, "there'll be full frankness, full openness, full honesty in our relationship." Bush reciprocated with "Russia and the United States are charting a new relationship, and it's based on trust; it's based on a commitment to economic and political freedom; it's based on a strong hope for true partnership."

Two decades later, when he met with a large group of foreigners and Russians at a conference in October 2014, Yeltsin's successor, Vladimir Putin, sounded very little like an old friend, college or otherwise. Scorn had replaced praise, as he lashed out at those who arrogantly called themselves the Cold War's "victors" and assumed that this gave them the right to "reshape the world to suit their own needs and interests" (Putin, 2014b). Barack Obama, he suggested, led a country that no longer knew how to "fight the real threats, such as regional conflicts, terrorism, drug trafficking, religious fanaticism, chauvinism, and neo-Nazism." Instead it had capitulated to "inflated national pride, manipulating public opinion, and letting the strong bully and suppress the weak." Obama, having earlier suggested that Putin was something less than a "genius" for having seized Crimea and embroiled Russia in the war in eastern Ukraine, in February 2015 responded with his own summary judgment: Mr Putin, he told a reporter, "has a foot very much in the Soviet past" (Obama, 2015).[1] He thinks like the KGB officer that he was; "he looks at problems through this Cold War lens." As a result, the president continued, "he's missed some opportunities for Russia to diversify its economy, to strengthen its relationship with its neighbors, to represent something different than the old Soviet-style aggression."

What on earth had happened? How could the two countries have arrived at a point so fundamentally different from the positive hopes expressed on that snowy day at Camp David in February 1992? A relationship this bleak and friction-laden normally has deep causes – some deep animus or historical enmity; an ideological irreconcilability or a grand geostrategic rivalry. The Cold War had more than one of these as its basis. But none of them figured in the post-Cold War US–Russian relationship. Over the years since the collapse of the Soviet Union, Washington and Moscow had had their clashes, and at times they had hurled angry words at each other, but nothing about either country had made it an anathema, a preoccupying threat, or an avowed enemy for the other. So, how had the two managed to lose control and send the relationship careening off the rails into a hostility that duplicated many characteristics of the Cold War?

The confrontation erupting around the deepening Ukrainian crisis obviously has been a defining factor – the moment when the train left the tracks – but to start or stop the explanation here would be to explain too little. Worse, it would narrow understanding to a near useless basis for figuring out how to pull the relationship out of its current depths and create something more civil and durably constructive. For the curious aspect of post-Cold War US–Russian relations and the feature that needs to be explained even before one turns to the reasons for the free-fall over Ukraine is the inability of the two sides ever to place the relationship on a self-sustaining basis, ever to find sturdy ground on which to build a progressively more fruitful relationship. Nothing has been more striking or frustrating about US–Russian relations over the last quarter century than the law-like rise and fall of expectations. Each time the two countries launched or relaunched a period promising increased cooperation, the momentum gradually faltered or events intervened to scuttle their progress and send the relationship spinning backward.

It would be a mistake, however, to think of this undulating curve as uniform and the ups and downs as similar from one occasion to the next. Looking back over these years, it is clear that the United States and Russia arrived where they are by stages. Each stage had its own distinctive qualities – its own successes, its own disappointments, and its own complexities; but the net effect, as one stage yielded to the next, was a slow descent toward a point where a dramatic turn of events, such as the confrontation over Ukraine, could send the relationship reeling.

Stages

When Boris Yeltsin returned to Washington four months after his initial meeting with Bush, he was there to lobby Congress and to sign a charter for American–Russian partnership and friendship. To call the document fulsome would be an impressive understatement, but this too was an artifact of the expectations guiding US and Russian leaders at the time – both real and rote. The reference to shared ideals of democracy and commitment to the rule of law, human rights, and fundamental freedoms may have been an honest aspiration on Yeltsin's part. It could only have been a hope on Bush's part. The reverse was probably true of the passage evoking their special responsibility as permanent members of the UN Security Council for maintaining international peace, and one can only guess what degree of conviction lay behind the loftier claim that together they would build "a democratic peace that unites the entire community of democratic nations" (White House Office of the Press Secretary, 1992).

Doubtless the soaring spirit of their declaration reflected a genuine sense of the grand possibilities opened by the revolutionary events that had just taken place. For Yeltsin, however, seizing the moment to give this vision concrete form was not his immediate priority. He and his foreign minister, Andrei Kozyrev, had decided that their country's fate lay with the West, and, to the condemnation of critics back home, they had embraced a "pro-Atlanticist" orientation. But this had far more to do with securing US support for the reform they were struggling to introduce in Russia than with co-managing a safer and more democratic world. Even the boldest actions Yeltsin proposed on the occasion – such as a steep cut in nuclear warheads to 2,500 for each country (from more than 9,000), the elimination of MIRV missiles, and a global missile defense system – were inspired more by an urgent need to reduce the country's defense burden than a deep desire to reduce the risk of nuclear war.

For the Bush administration, now convinced of Yeltsin's democratic bona fides, his success was seen as important, but it was an election year, the US economy was in recession, and there was resistance in both the administration and Congress to investing heavily in his success. Historic as the opportunity might have been, key figures in the administration, including the president, focused more on the risks entailed in the momentous but chaotic change underway. First among these was what was to happen to the vast Soviet nuclear arsenal now spread across four newly independent, but shaky states. The bulk of these holdings remained in Russia, but the numbers elsewhere were formidable. In Kazakhstan, for example, the quantity of nuclear warheads nearly totaled those held today by the United States. The other near-term priority was to help cushion the pain that the collapse was inflicting on the Russian population, lest it lead to public unrest threatening Yeltsin's reforms. So, food aid to avert feared starvation over the 1991-2 winter flowed, and so did advice from a host of official and semi-official advisors on how to build democratic institutions and a functioning market. Large-scale assistance buttressing the reform effort itself – such as for currency stabilization and debt relief – however, was not part of the picture.

The incoming Clinton administration shared the Bush administration's sense that Boris Yeltsin represented Russia's best hope for replacing what had been an ugly reality – and still could be another – with a democratic future. Indeed, Clinton and his people took the proposition much further, because a far more elaborate set of assumptions shaped their notion of Russia's role in US foreign policy. Russia was seen as key to outcomes throughout the former Soviet Union: reform there would enable it elsewhere; failure there would produce failure elsewhere. Even more to the point, Russia transformed would usher in a world where the United States no longer need be preoccupied with nuclear "what ifs," with fattening its defense budget, and with the other pathologies of the Cold War. But, if Russia faltered, if Yeltsin fell, all these benefits would be lost, and the United States would be back to large-scale defense spending and contending with renewed international tensions. Not to mention, were chaos to ensue, as Clinton warned, the United States would be facing "the strife of the former Yugoslavia replicated in a nation as big as Russia, spanning eleven time zones with an armed arsenal of nuclear weapons that is still very vast" (Clinton, 1993). Russia should be a preoccupation now, because, "if it blew up in our face," it would certainly become a preoccupation.

The syllogism was large, powerful, and simple – in great part, too simple. Many in the administration – none more than the president – accepted the idea that democracies do not go to war against one another, and, if Russia could make that transition, it would provide a crucial impetus to a more peaceful world. The chance of its making that transition, however, depended on Yeltsin and his team. If they succumbed to the mounting opposition at home (and Clinton had concluded even before entering the White House that Yeltsin was "up to his ass in alligators"), the likely alternative was an unreconstructed Communist Party, wounded but not yet defeated, or a macédoine of nationalists and neo-fascists (Talbott, 2002, p. 38). Hence the administration's highest priority, with the president driving it harder than anyone, was to do everything possible to back Yeltsin and the reformers with as much economic, technical, and political help as they could muster.

Understandably, on the other side, Yeltsin's stake in the relationship came down largely to rallying the United States behind the revolution he was struggling to work within Russia. Without that support – material and political – said his foreign minister, Andrei Kozyrev, to a senior US diplomat in late 1992, as the angry opposition to the reforms swelled, "we're finished" (Talbott, 2002, p. 41). Yeltsin's aggressive pro-Western/pro-American posture was doubtless sincere; it constituted an external identity consistent with the country he wanted Russia to be, and it had the secondary advantage of ingratiating his government with countries whose support he desperately sought. But it was the product of impulse, not of vision. It was without clear conceptual content, without thought of how and to what degree Russia was to be integrated with the West, when almost certainly it could not be integrated into the West's institutions. Adding to its vulnerability, the impulse aroused deep antipathy among significant portions of the Russian political and military elite.

One sympathizes with leaders trying to keep their footing amid this crushing rush of events, but, unnoticed, pupating in the underside of the events that had their attention were three hazards that, when they matured, would carry the relationship, stage by stage, through the descent. The first of these, Yeltsin's reforms, preoccupied both sides, but the reformers gave too little attention to building the necessary political base for them, and the administration, while nervous about the neglect, did too little to act on it. A stark biramous calculation governed their thinking: either Yeltsin would succeed or reform would fail. The likelihood of something in between and the challenges that would pose figured only faintly, until the crisis surrounding reform literally exploded in the violent siege of the parliament in fall 1993. As a result the two defects that would eventually paralyze Russia's progress toward democracy and a well-functioning market, while at the same time pumping toxins into the US–Russian relationship – namely, reform's missing political foundation and its susceptibility to monumental corruption – were treated by both sides as secondary problems, not the very essence of the matter.

Second, two harbingers of what from the beginning represented the deadliest threat to the hoped-for historic partnership also escaped notice – or, at least, active attention. Over the years that followed, nothing battered ties between the two countries more than the destructive interaction between Russia's heavy-handed behavior in the post-Soviet space and the United States contested role there. Early shoots of the problem appeared in the balky way Russia went about closing facilities and removing its troops from the three Baltic states. For both the Bush and Clinton administrations, the dithering introduced strain into the relationship and, ultimately, in the Estonian case, a threat from the Clinton administration to cut off all support for reform unless Russia met the agreed deadline. Getting the troops out was the immediate problem, but not its larger, lethal core. That resided in the Yeltsin leadership's unreadiness from the start, before the issue hardened, to set about rectifying history and striving to build a relationship with these and other new neighbors inspiring comity rather than fear, one eschewing coercion in favor of trust-building. Nor on the US side was this a course either urged or facilitated with any particular passion.

The other foul straw in the wind originated in the violent conflicts that erupted as the Soviet Union broke apart – in Moldova, Azerbaijan, Georgia, and Tajikistan. Early in the Clinton administration, Russian leaders were prepared to work together with the United States in attempting to extinguish or, short of that, cap what eventually would evolve into the "frozen" or protracted conflicts that now pock the geography of the region and that, at key points, have added to the frictions in US–Russian relations. And initially the Clinton administration began to develop a policy to do just that. But in October 1993, after a firefight in Somalia and the bodies of dead marines were dragged through the streets of Mogadishu, opposition to do-good US interventions boiled forth on the pages of the *Wall Street Journal* and in Congress, and the administration buried its plans. Meanwhile, the Russians, their gaze turning from the excitement of their new relationship with the West to the troubles in the post-Soviet region, jettisoned their interest in cooperating with the outside world and demanded that they be deputized by the UN as the agent responsible for the region's security. Trouble lay ahead.

The third shadow creeping across the relationship, and an early sign of the ills that would contaminate its next stage and those to follow, arose in the Balkans. By 1993 Slobodan Milošević's brutal war in Bosnia had grown considerably more brutal; the United States was arguing strenuously for stiffer retaliation; and Russia was having none of it. Yeltsin's recalcitrance stemmed primarily from political calculation: the Serbs' cause was popular in Russia, particularly among the opposition and within the military, and he was persuaded that backing US-led military actions would risk losing an impeachment vote that loomed ahead. As reported by Strobe Talbott, Clinton's senior Russian advisor, another less open, but more insidious factor was also at work. In conversations between Talbott and Vladimir Lukin, the Russian ambassador in Washington, who was no hawk or crude nationalist, the latter voiced the suspicion that the exercise against the Serbs ("anti-Serb vendetta," he called it) was a dry run for further NATO incursions, including into the space around Russia (Talbott, 2002, p. 77). Mistrust whose lineage traced back directly to the Cold War thus began to make its reappearance soon into the new era. Moreover, if it survived within a liberal such as Lukin, how much more virulent was it in more conservative segments of the Russian political establishment. Similarly, during the tense and difficult negotiations over the removal of nuclear weapons from Ukraine, Yevgeny Primakov, then the head of the

Russian Foreign Intelligence Service, as Talbott recounts, suggested that the "real motive for America's 'generous offer of assistance' was to lure Ukraine into a US-led camp that would 'encircle Russia with our former fraternal republics and allies'" (ibid., p. 80).

Throughout these years, efforts to move relations forward were buffeted by a series of problems that had the potential of derailing the whole undertaking. First came the controversy over the Russian decision to sell cryogenic technology to the Indian space agency, a violation of the Missile Technology Control Regime (MTCR) of which Russia was a part; the still more disconcerting eagerness of Rosatom to supply Iran with a light water nuclear reactor; and finally, by late 1994, Russia's war in Chechnya. Most notably in all of these cases the two governments were able to maneuver through the difficulty – in some instances, as with the Indian space agency, by carrots and cajoling on the US part; in others, as with Iran, by finding a format for extending the discussion; and, in the case of Chechnya, by Clinton's decision to hold his nose and rationalize the war as a justified step to keep the country whole (he even, to the dismay of his advisors, compared Yeltsin's action to Lincoln's choice in the American Civil War). The point, however, is that the two sides were able to surmount these road-blocks, because both wanted to do so and willingly sought workable compromises. Added to the very real accomplishments of these early years – a radically advanced strategic nuclear arms control agreement, the de-nuclearization of Belarus, Kazakhstan, and Ukraine, and the Cooperative Threat Reduction program to safely reduce and secure nuclear weapons in Russia – this stage in US–Russian relations was not merely hope-filled, but hope fulfilled, and the two countries had every reason to assume that the progress would continue.

In faltering fashion it did. Washington and Moscow, however, were now entering a period marked by developments more fateful than either realized. None was more fraught than the decision to add to NATO the former Warsaw Pact states of Hungary, Poland, and the Czech Republic, an idea that began bubbling in various quarters in 1993 and for the next year and a half percolated fitfully in US–Russian relations. Yeltsin and those around him were from the start alarmed by talk of NATO enlargement but partially reassured by the uncertainty within the administration over how soon this might happen. The uncertainty owed partly to divisions among senior officials over how to proceed and partly to their strained attempt to find a format and compensations that would reconcile the Russians to enlargement when it came.

Reconciliation never happened, despite the special NATO–Russia charter concluded simultaneously with the admission of new members into NATO. Like acid eating away the struts beneath the two sides' diplomatic efforts in a war-ravaged Bosnia, their search for a compromise propping up a fraying European conventional arms control regime, and their attempts to contain Moscow's explosive anger over the US-led 1999 Kosovo War, Russia's lingering hostility to NATO persisted and, in fact, gathered strength in the following decade as tensions over NATO's role in the post-Soviet space, its interventions "out-of-area," and its plans to deploy missile defense mounted. Here too the legacy of the Cold War lived on vibrantly and with ever more destructive force.[2]

The NATO decision was a critical turning point in the post-Cold War evolution of US–Russian – indeed, Russian–West – relations, but for a reason different from the reasons that have dominated the debate between the decision's critics and defenders. On one side, George Kennan, when in 1997 still hoping NATO would reconsider plans to enlarge, predicted what many say has happened. "Expanding NATO," he wrote in a *New York Times* op-ed piece, would be the most fateful error of American policy in the entire post-cold war era. Such a decision may be expected to inflame the nationalist, anti-Western and militaristic tendencies in Russian opinion; to have an adverse effect on the development of Russian democracy; to restore the atmosphere of the cold war in East–West relations, and to impel Russian foreign policy in directions decidedly not to our liking. (Kennan, 1997)

Those who defended the original decision argued then, and do so now, that extending NATO's sphere in Europe was never intended as a threat to Russia but as a wise step toward ensuring that a "grey zone" or security vacuum did not emerge in Europe's center, providing a way to resolve the historical tension between Poland and Germany, and serving as a vehicle for bringing democracy and economic reform to these new members.

Kennan was right. So, were those on the other side. Thus, the debate ended in irreconcilable truths, bringing to mind Nils Bohr's observation that "the opposite of a correct statement is a false statement. But the opposite of a profound truth may well be another profound truth." Both, however, miss the larger tragedy so central to the puzzle of why Russia and the United States have not been able to build a durably cooperative relationship and why the underlying trend in their relations has been the descent into today's confrontation.

The hard reality is that neither side ever truly tried to build the comprehensive, integrated European security system that their vaulted rhetoric promised at the end of the Cold War, rhetoric regularly repeated in speeches and documents of the OSCE as late as the OSCE heads of state summit in 2010. Now no longer. If Russia, the European states, and the United States had seriously contemplated creating what they so glibly spoke of and no doubt genuinely wished for, the security problem they would have had to solve was that of Ukraine. In solving that, they would have solved the problem of a security vacuum in Central Europe. Solving that, however, would have required devising arrangements acceptable to Russia. By solving one half of Europe's security problem through NATO enlargement, they accentuated the security problem in Europe's other half and laid waste to the prospect of creating a broader Euro-Atlantic security community.

It need not have been that way even with – indeed, preferably with – a vital NATO. During the debate within the administration in 1995-6, Secretary of Defense William Perry, in shades of George Kennan 1949-50, resisted the idea of an early expansion of NATO and argued for first getting the NATO–Russia relationship right and, in the meantime, giving the intermediate arrangement with non-NATO members, the Partnership for Peace, a chance to work (Goldgeier and McFaul, 2003, p. 195). An integral as opposed to a partial European security system would have required a functioning partnership between Russia and NATO, not one that was merely nominal, together with security arrangements – bilateral as well as multilateral – that assured the "new lands in between" their security.

Accomplishing that did not depend only on the choices the United States and NATO were making during these years. Russia bears equal if not greater responsibility for the failure of what could and should have been. No version of Europe whole and secure was or is possible unless Russia's neighbors are comfortable in its shadow. Had the Yeltsin leadership truly wished to prevent NATO enlargement and produce a security environment more congenial to their country, they would have much sooner stopped taking their new neighbors for granted or, worse, derogating their sovereignty and featuring sticks over carrots and worked hard to establish Russia as a trustworthy security partner, not merely for NATO, but for all those states located between

NATO and Russia. Not that it would have been easy, but had Russia from the beginning invested heavily in softening the hardened views of Eastern Europeans and the new post-Soviet states and labored earnestly to build a constructive, respectful relationship with them, the pressure to enlarge NATO would have been less, and the thought of doing so, absent in Washington and Brussels in 1991, would likely have remained so.

This now damaged framework, the surviving alternative to the one promised – the only one, in all likelihood, that would have provided the underpinning preventing US–Russian relations from experiencing the ups and downs that lay ahead – formed the carapace within which Russian and US leaders shaped their response to the opportunities and obstacles arising over the next decade and a half. Six years later another dimension further warped the relationship, when in 2003 President Putin began to veer sharply from Russia's previous, rather wobbly transition to democracy. Before that, and before a new president arrived in the White House, in Clinton and Yeltsin's last two years in office relations slipped into a certain desuetude, less an enterprise seen as a failure than one shorn of the exuberant expectations that had characterized Clinton's first years in the presidency. In 1998 Kozyrev's decidedly unromantic successor, Yevgeny Primakov, long past the notion of "pro-Atlanticist" solidarity, began drumming on the theme of a multipolar world in which Russia, China, and India should make common cause. His American counterpart, Madeleine Albright, unsettled by the backsliding on the Russian side, noted that until now the two countries "had been able to advance our cooperation where our interests converge and to manage our differences honestly and constructively," but, she added, "the question now is whether that cooperation can continue" (Albright, 1998, p. 194). Six months later, at the height of the Kosovo crisis, Yeltsin's Russia in full throat angrily denounced NATO's military assault on Milošević's forces, walked away from the Permanent Joint Council – the sop to Russia at the time of NATO enlargement that Moscow had never much cared for – and began running military exercises designed to counter operations like that NATO had just carried out in Kosovo.

George W. Bush came to office as the first US president in post-World War II history without a Russia policy and critical of the Clinton administration for having one described, by Condoleezza Rice, his senior foreign policy advisor, as too ready to accommodate the Russians, too personalized, and too given to "happy talk" (Rice, 2000, pp. 57–60). Within a year he was deeply engaged with Putin's Russia, and during the next eight years he would preside over the sharpest rise and fall in US–Russian relations of any period in the post-Cold War era until the present.

The attack on the World Trade Center in September 2001 launched the rapid ascent of the relationship. Over the next two years, beginning with Putin's swift and firm support following 9/11, Russia's quiet retreat when the administration discarded the ABM treaty in December 2001, its assistance in the Afghan war against the Taliban, and ending in Rome in May 2002 with the redo of the NATO–Russian relationship and the creation of the NATO–Russia Council (NRC), ties between the countries reached a level of accord unmatched since the early years of the first Clinton administration. The US ambassador in Moscow, Alexander Vershbow, even spoke of a strategic alliance between the two countries and, after the formation of the NRC, of an "alliance with an alliance."[3]

Putin, for his part, not only rallied to the United States after the 9/11 terrorist attack, okayed military bases for US and coalition forces in Central Asia, and aided in the war against the Taliban, but praised collaboration with the United States as in basic Russian interest. When speaking to the Washington press before heading to Bush's Crawford ranch in November 2001, he enthusiastically reported that "Today we are already prepared to seek solutions in all areas of our joint activities. We are willing to dismantle, once and for all, the legacy of the Cold War and begin fashioning a strategic partnership for the long-term" (Putin, 2001). During the same period he frequently noted Russia's European identity and the integral connection of Russian with European culture.

A shadow, however, hung over the renewed optimism of the early 2000s. Little could leaders in the two countries have anticipated how quickly the arc of optimism would crest and plummet. Not that the Bush administration had ignored the repressive measures the Putin leadership had taken in Russia, its conduct of the Chechen War, and its less than gentle approach in disputes with its new neighbors. And not that Putin had failed to make plain those aspects of US policy of which he was less than enamored. But neither understood the potential damaging force from the underlayment of misgivings and mistrust that had been building since the mid-1990s, and which neither they nor their predecessors had addressed, doubtless because none recognized what was forming at the deeper level.

When the clouds blackened in 2003 and seriously disruptive events intervened, the underlayment greatly magnified the effects. May 2002 marked the high water mark for the second energized US–Russian effort to put the relationship on a constructive track. That month the United States and Russia signed the Strategic Offensive Reductions Treaty (SORT), reducing another tranche of deployed nuclear warheads, and with NATO members set up the NATO–Russia Council, giving Russia a more equal voice in joint deliberations. Within short order, however, the progress achieved over the previous two years was battered by the near simultaneous intrusion of three developments that now emerged as the principal negative drivers in the relationship.

The havoc they caused dictated the downward curve of relations for the remainder of Bush's term in office.

First came the United States' rush to war in Iraq in March 2003. Russia had supported the US–NATO war in Afghanistan. In contrast the Iraq War solidified a view that had been slowly congealing since the 1999 Kosovo War. The United States, Putin and his people concluded, too often and too recklessly permitted itself to intervene with military force whenever and wherever it pleased, while paying little attention to the views and concerns of others. Second, six months later, a terrorist attack on a school in Beslan, a town in Russia's north Caucasus, that led to a heavy loss in lives, most of them children, ended with Putin's sharp tightening of political control within Russia – muzzling political opposition, shrinking the room for civic action, cracking down on the media, and centralizing political control. Before 2003 the Bush administration had left to the side the political abuses that they knew were accumulating, but the sudden clenching of the iron fist brought the issue to the fore. By the time Bush met Putin in Bratislava, Slovakia, in February 2005, he had already begun publicly airing his misgivings, and at their summit he now confronted his Russian counterpart over them. Putin and his colleagues responded rather like their Soviet predecessors: "It is none of your business." However, because, unlike their predecessors, they still insisted that Russia shared Western political values, they then invented notions such as "sovereign democracy" to justify their "managed" version.

The third development eventually evolved into the most destructive of the three. In November 2003, the first of three color revolutions imploded in Georgia. As would be the case in Ukraine a year later and in Kyrgyzstan in 2005, it was driven by a rebellion against massive corruption and manipulated elections. All three toppled regimes, and in Georgia and Ukraine they brought to power leaders distinctly unpalatable to Moscow. Moscow portrayed this turn of events not as a pot that boiled over on its own but as the handiwork of agents from the outside. It was the embryo of a poisonous notion that emerged in full form a decade later as the two countries descended into the new Cold War. Years later, when looking back over intervening events, Putin and his closest advisors convinced themselves that the United States had not simply stumbled into Iraq, Libya, and Syria but had been pursuing a conscious, systematic strategy of regime change as a means of achieving larger strategic objectives. Ukraine was the latest and boldest instance, with in this case Russia as the target.

For the Russian side, the converging effect of these three increasingly inflamed sources of tension culminated in Putin's performance before a stunned audience at the 2007 Munich Security Conference. In one thunderous paroxysm of displeasure he united his various criticisms from the past and hurled the collected mass at the United States – in the first instance at Robert Gates, Bush's secretary of defense, who was seated in the front row before him. The United States, he argued, mistakenly thinks it operates in a unipolar world, disdains the "basic principles of international law," pushes NATO ever closer to Russian borders, contrary to earlier promises, uses the OSCE to interfere in Russia's internal affairs, and engages in "almost uncontained hyper use of force" (Putin, 2007). For the US side, the culmination came one year later, when in August 2008 Russia sent its army into Georgia, occupied the two separatist regions of Abkhazia and South Ossetia, and then, with precious little support even from allies, recognized them as independent states. What began as one of the high points in post-Cold War US–Russian relations ended at their lowest point.

From these depths, the Obama administration undertook for the third time to resurrect the relationship and put it on a more solid footing. This time, however, the easy optimism of earlier interludes was absent. Indeed, at the outset, among Putin, his team, and much of the Russian establishment, little will existed to struggle with finding ways to improve matters. It was Barack Obama, somewhat to the surprise of his senior advisors, who made Russia an early priority, along with the Afghan War and Iran's nuclear program, and then invited the Russians to join in "resetting" US–Russian relations. Three months into his presidency, he met with Russia's new president, Dmitri Medvedev, in London, and the two outlined a bold new agenda that ranged from revitalizing stalled strategic arms control efforts to launching a "comprehensive dialogue" on European security, and from finding new approaches to mutual energy security to addressing a host of concrete issues, such as Russia's WTO membership, a fissile material cutoff treaty, and ratification of the Comprehensive Nuclear Test Ban Treaty (CTBT).

Much of this eventually fell by the wayside: the largest and most ambitious topics, such as a serious dialogue over European security, were soon eclipsed by the immediate problems of the day; others, such as ratification of the CTBT, ran into a US congressional roadblock, and the fissile material cutoff treaty remained hostage to Pakistan's veto. In any event, while the two countries went about beefing up the relationship with practical forms of cooperation, including an impressive set of working groups under the US–Russian Bilateral Presidential Commission established three months after the London meeting, the administration focused its attention on four key tasks – four tasks that reflected the priority given to Russia, Afghanistan, and Iran, and that would serve as the administration's benchmarks for judging the success of the "reset."[4]

Russia was a priority, because managing nuclear weapons was the number one foreign policy objective that Obama identified even during his presidential campaign, and it figured in two of the four tasks: first, salvaging the Strategic Arms Limitation Treaty, set to expire in December 2009, and, second, enlisting Russia in what would be Obama's new initiative to convene an international summit committing states to tighter controls over nuclear materials. Third, the administration sought Russian cooperation in creating a supply route to the Afghan War that came from the north across Russia. And, fourth, in addressing the Iranian nuclear issue, the administration wanted Russia's backing in tightening UN sanctions on Teheran.

Thus, the Obama administration had a strategic agenda. So did the Russian leadership, one driven by the economic crisis of 2008-9, a crisis that hit Russia much harder than most countries, including its BRICS partners. By fall 2009 Medvedev and Putin - albeit with different emphases - had begun stressing the urgency of modernizing Russia's economy. If modernization was the priority, then "What we need," Medvedev said in a speech to an assembly of Russian ambassadors in July 2010, "are special modernization alliances with our main international partners. And who are they? First of all, it is countries such as Germany, France, Italy, the European Union in general, and the United States" (Medvedev, 2010). While Europe would be the partner of scale, little progress would be achieved without the blessing and commitment of the United States.

More than a strategic agenda, the Obama administration also gradually arrived at a strategic conception on how to build the relationship, something none of the three previous US administrations had managed to do. Though not often touted in these terms, it featured a multidimensional, multilevel approach - multidimensional by emphasizing the importance of generating more ballast for relations than simply that of cooperation on strategic arms control, important as this was. Economic ties, cooperation in promoting technological innovation, and addressing new global challenges, such as climate change, would create a sounder and more well-rounded foundation. By multilevel, the administration meant that the relationship should depend not only on government-to-government contact but also on flourishing connections between business communities and civil society.[5] There is no indication that the Russian side had a counterpart strategic conception, but it appeared to have no trouble embracing that of the administration, albeit grudgingly when it came to discussing the role of civil society in Russia.

The crucial missing piece for both sides – in fairness, a piece missing from the policy of all previous leaderships – was a strategic vision for the relationship. It need simply have been a notion of what each side wanted the relationship to be five or six years down the road; what each thought might be realistically accomplished over that period in areas where each had a vital role to play; and what obstacles stood in the way. And then the two sides would have needed to share their visions, decide where they were compatible, and set about pursuing them.

Its absence would haunt the slow crumbling of relations and then their precipitous collapse over the next four years. Achieving the four goals on the administration's strategic agenda had not been easy, but by late spring 2010, with the signing of New START, they had been largely fulfilled, and the Obama team turned their minds to moving beyond the reset, giving their efforts a new wind, and making a partnership for modernization and technological innovation a promising new focus. They failed. The reset had no sequel. Instead, as a number of events that set the two sides at odds intervened, the three corrosive grievances that came to a head during the last two-thirds of the Bush administration re-entered with still more insidious force.

Just as the friction-filled year 2003 merged and magnified their effect, 2011 did the same – only more so. It began in March with the

US-backed intervention in Libya, an action that Moscow had facilitated when the goal was to prevent genocide in the eastern half of
the country but condemned when it turned to ousting the Gaddafi
regime. On the heels of the Libyan intervention, the US campaign
against Bashar al-Assad in the Syrian civil war was perceived as more
of the United States recklessly toppling regimes without considering
the chaos that would follow. At this point the Putin regime, in its anger
over unilateral US military interventions and propensity for regime
change, lumped the two together; the Ukrainian crisis separated them
and transformed the issue of regime change into the badly warped
notion that the United States had acted not as a matter of poor policy
choices, but in pursuit of a conscious strategy – hence, making it a
distinct, grave, and direct threat to Russia. The administration in turn
grew ever more convinced that Russia was now bent on stirring up
trouble wherever it promised to create problems for the United States
or, in the Syrian case, seeking short-term gains with no regard for the
Assad regime's role in a barbarous war.

That winter popular demonstrations erupted in Russia's major
cities following parliamentary elections that were seen as a charade
underwriting an outcome decided elsewhere. They shook the regime
and prompted steps to ensure nothing comparable would happen
in the upcoming presidential election. A shrill anti-American media
campaign was one of them, including Putin's spokesman's allegation
that Secretary of State Hillary Clinton had played a role in instigat-
ing the December post-election protests. It turned out that the heavy
hand was more than electoral politics: when the political tightening
continued with further repressive measures, such as harsh constraints
on non-governmental organizations and the harassment of political
opposition – and no letup of anti-Americanism in the media – the
Obama administration's increasingly unfavorable view of Putin and

the government he commanded added to the weight the relationship now bore.

One issue, however, reflected the debilitating impact of the underlying burdens on the relationship more strikingly than any other. US plans to deploy a missile defense system in Europe, principally as a counter to a potential Iranian nuclear threat, had stirred Russian opposition from the beginning. The Obama administration's decision to undo the original plan to place key portions of the system in Poland and the Czech Republic, coupled with the warming atmosphere during the reset, however, allowed the two sides at the Lisbon NATO–Russia Council meeting in November 2010, attended by President Medvedev, to agree on the need to find a cooperative approach to the issue. Leaders on both sides recognized, as Vice-President Biden would say in a Moscow speech in March 2011, that agreement on missile defense would be a political "game-changer," fundamentally altering NATO members' framing of the Russian security challenge and Russia's perception of the NATO threat (Biden, 2011).

Negotiations began, and for two years they ground on, making little headway and doing little to lessen the accusations of bad faith and obstructionism that each regularly leveled at the other. A completely integrated joint Russian–European missile defense system was never contemplated, but the real-time coordination of separate systems was not unrealistic, and a high-level group of former US, European, and Russian foreign and defense policy officials did manage to work out the details of such a system.[6] In the politics of the day, however, with accommodation fiercely opposed by the Russian defense and security establishment and by arms control opponents in the US Congress, the negotiations simply trod water. In the end the game changer was never given a chance. Ultimately, the legacy of mistrust carried the day. On the Russian side, the sterile image of NATO, gingered by anger over its movement toward Russian borders, claimed another victim. If the failure did not turn out to be a game spoiler, that was because the game was spoiled by another development.

The Ukrainian Crisis

The post-Cold War museum of "could've/should've beens" contains something basic that did not happen. Had Ukraine (and, by extension, Belarus and Moldova) early on been encouraged to pursue what an economist would call a risk-averting strategy rather than a balancing strategy, there would be no Ukrainian crisis. That is, had Ukrainian leaders sought close and constructive relations both with the East and with the West, rather than vacillating over alignment with only one side, history would never have ended in Russia's annexation of Crimea, the war in eastern Ukraine, the crisis of the Ukrainian economy, and a Russia–West confrontation. But, for Ukraine to follow that path, Russia, the United States and Europe would have had to make it possible. Making it possible would have required that, as a first-order priority, they subordinate their specific hopes for Ukraine to outcomes reconciling these with those of the other side. More specifically, that would have meant devising ways by which Ukraine could benefit from the economic integration projects of both East and West, and, together, East and West would both strengthen Ukrainian security. Had Russia, Europe, and the United States been seriously pursuing the larger Euro-Atlantic security vision that they kept talking about, this would have been a component part.

Was the Ukrainian crisis avoidable? Maybe. But only with a prescience and capacity for introspection that none of the parties had. Historians will be the ones to make sense of it. On the one hand, they will doubtless be puzzled, because there is little logic to the collapse of US–Russian relations. On the other hand, they are the ones who specialize in explaining, with the benefit of hindsight, how flawed narratives, political missteps, and the unexpected event produce history-changing outcomes. Surely, however, they will agree that Russia's actions in Crimea and the Donbas were the cause that sent the relationship sailing over the cliff. The challenge will be to untangle the reasons Russia chose to act as it did, which will in turn present the larger challenge of reconstructing the complex interaction produced by the choices of all sides – US, European, and Russian – and the calculations, including the miscalculations, behind them.

Viktor Yanukovych's sudden decision in November 2013 to back out of a laboriously negotiated free trade agreement with the EU started things. Known as an Association Agreement, the arrangement aimed to draw Ukraine closer to Europe economically while fostering more European-like practices in the country. When that opportunity was tossed aside, outraged citizens – in particular, the young – took to the streets. What followed had a long and involved lead-up in which the grievances and encrusted biases accumulating since the mid-1990s played a central role.

While Russia from the start had strongly opposed NATO's expansion eastward, it had been more relaxed as the EU added new members, even when enlargement included the three Baltic states. This began to change after 2003, when the EU, ten countries larger, moved to develop the European Neighborhood Policy (ENP), a plan intended to create opportunities, short of membership, for countries on its eastern and southern borders. When, five years later, Poland, joined by Sweden, pushed to create the Eastern Partnership, a project expressly designed to enhance the EU's relationship with Belarus, Ukraine, Moldova, Georgia, Azerbaijan, and Armenia, Russian attitudes hardened. These were also the years of gathering tensions in US–Russian relations, and, to the extent that Russia viewed developments in Europe through the lens of its evolving relationship with Washington, EU actions took on further shades of meaning.

The EU's Eastern Partnership, adopted in 2009, reflected two impulses, only one of which mattered to the Russian side. For most EU members it, like the ENP of which it was part, was a casually embraced gesture intended to pacify states that wanted in to the EU but that would not be given that chance, while minimizing a potentially sharp dividing line between members and nearby non-members. Russia was not the target. Russia, in fact, was not even part of the calculation. For the Poles and other new members on the EU's eastern edge, however, the Eastern Partnership had a deeper significance. By drawing Ukraine and others closer to the EU and encouraging economic and political change facilitating their cooperation with the EU, they sought to create a buffer diluting their own exposure to their large neighbor to the east. This was the impulse that mattered to Moscow.

In the meantime, over the same period, Russia's long-sputtering efforts to draw together parts of the former Soviet Union into some kind of trading bloc gathered momentum. From 2007 on, Putin put increasing stress on actually welding these states (Belarus, Kazakhstan, and Kyrgyzstan) into a functioning customs union as the first step toward more ambitious levels of integration. And in 2011 he unveiled plans for a fully integrated Eurasian Economic Union, Russia's bid to create its own regional economic bloc, allowing it to keep up in a world of increasingly powerful regional economic blocs. Earlier in 2003, Putin and his EU counterparts spoke of coordinating their respective economic undertakings and creating between them a "common economic space." Putin, at that point, introduced the idea of a Europe economically united from "Lisbon to Vladivostok," a phrase he repeated regularly over the next ten years. By 2008, however, it was becoming clear that the future was for dueling, not coordinated, integration projects, and Ukraine was caught between.

In 2007, before the Eastern Partnership was in place, Ukraine had begun negotiating a special trading arrangement with the EU. For the next several years it was an off-and-on affair, as Ukrainian leaders struggled with the comprehensive reforms the Association Agreement would require, while fending off Russian pressure to join the Russian-sponsored customs union without closing the door to some form of cooperation. When finally in 2012 it appeared the EU deal had finally been done, the Russians grew increasingly anxious. By November 2013, as the date for signing loomed, they were in full checkmate mode, preying on Yanukovych's easily stimulated reluctance to make the concessions the Association Agreement would have required and countering with substantial economic offers to a Ukraine in deep economic trouble. Putin appeared motivated by the mounting apprehension – however unrealistic – that the EU, in Ukraine's case, was simply a stalking horse for forces determined to bring the country into NATO. He also appears to have been influenced by those around him, including an economic advisor, Sergey Glaziev, who argued vociferously that the EU–Ukraine Association Agreement would inflict untold harm on Russia's economic stakes in Ukraine. Many have also argued, probably with merit, that Ukraine lost to Putin's plans for the Eurasian Union – not that its membership was ever a likely prospect – would devastate if not doom these plans. In any event, Russia's fevered response to a Ukrainian move whose likely outcome had no better prospect than the EU and NATO's prior agreements with Ukraine was over-determined.

Yanukovych's abrupt about-face and the eruption of public protests that followed, however, do not explain the swift convulsion of events that sent the US–Russian relationship over the edge. Russia's annexation of Crimea and the subsequent chain of events flowed from a sequence of unanticipated occurrences, bringing to a fine point all of the frustrations and grievances, some badly malformed, slowly coalescing over the previous decade. Had the Ukrainian regime responded to the December protests with restraint, the popular ire probably would have eventually flagged and the public's resignation returned. The police violence against youthful demonstrators, followed a month later by crudely repressive legislation passed in the Rada, transformed a protest against a government action into a revolution against a regime whose corruption and incompetence provided plenty of cause.

When next the Yanukovych government shook and then cracked, agreeing under the pressure of events and the intervention of German, French, and Polish foreign ministers to negotiate an arrangement restoring the 2004 constitution, trimming presidential powers, and bringing forward new presidential elections to no later than the end of the year, the opposition leadership no longer controlled the streets. Yanukovych, for reasons still not entirely explained, fled, and the deal hung helplessly suspended. Historians will come back to the seventy-two hours between the massacre on the Maidan the night of February 20, the deal worked out on the 21st, Yanukovych's flight that night, and, within hours, the formation of an interim government drawn from opposition forces, including elements of the far right. They turned history's page. Putin's decision – and it was his – to seize control of Crimea was taken in the twelve hours between the unraveling of the deal and the appearance of Ukraine's new government, although contingency planning for it had long been underway.

Understanding his action leads back to the miasma of anger and suspicion collecting within Putin and his circle the decade before.[7]

Convinced that whatever room for maneuver Russia had had in Ukraine's encumbered political environment had vanished in a stroke, and that power had fallen, with US and European connivance, into the hands of unambiguously anti-Russia forces likely to tie Ukraine as close as possible to NATO, he struck, grasping the handiest lever available to him. Annexation appears to have been a separate decision, taken only when he decided that a lever – more a stick in the spokes of Ukraine's political momentum – was not enough, and that Russia dared not risk losing strategic control over its vital bridgehead on the Black Sea. Indulging the emotional satisfaction of retrieving Crimea for Russia and making its recovery a centerpiece of an increasingly nationalistic political appeal back home followed, rather than preceded, his actions.

Stunned by what they saw as a bald move by a major European power to grab by force a slice of another country, a country whose territorial integrity it had guaranteed, in disdain for what the West believed to be a core norm of the European order, whatever its rationale, prompted an instant and far-reaching response. In the case of the Obama administration, Russian actions in Crimea catapulted US–Russian relations into a fourth and ultimate stage of decline. The president had begun with the hopes inspiring the reset and, after considerable success in the first two years, grew increasingly frustrated as the effort to advance beyond the reset bogged down, until in fall 2013 he canceled his summit with Putin and took Russia off his desk, leaving it to his foreign and defense secretaries to make what progress they could. The paralyzed negotiations on missile defense and the refuge given Edward Snowden were the last straw. The United States, he said, was "taking a pause" in the relationship. Ukraine ended the pause. Russia was very much back on Obama's desk, only this time not as an opportunity but as a serious challenge.

Meanwhile, Russia seized on the resistance that events in Kiev had stirred in Ukraine's eastern provinces and began fanning the flames of separatism in Donetsk and Lugansk. In what came to be known as the "Novorossiya Project" – Novorossiya, Imperial Russia's name for the Ukrainian territory north of the Black Sea – Putin apparently persuaded himself that the Russian diaspora in eastern Ukraine, as in the Crimea, would, with Russian assistance, throw off Ukrainian authority. Whether he thought this would lead to the formation of independent entities in the two provinces or spread beyond to the other eastern provinces, let alone end with annexation by Russia, is not clear. Because the idea came to him late and in the rush of events, quite likely he was not thinking that far ahead. At a minimum, however, buttressing separatist forces in the east had the useful function of keeping the new government in Kiev and its Western sponsors off balance. More than that, in the months that followed, the tumult of war deepened Ukraine's economic crisis and, for the EU and NATO, transformed the country from an opportunity into a burden.

As the war dragged on with ever deeper Russian involvement, including a direct (although denied) Russian military operation to rescue the separatists from military defeat in late summer 2014, the new Cold War emerged in full form. The Europeans, including most notably Angela Merkel's Germany, concluded, as had the Obama administration, that Russia was not simply a difficult partner but now an unpredictable threat and, unless compelled to change course, capable of wrecking the post-Cold War European security order.

Viewed from Moscow, Ukraine was the final proof that the United States was bent on marginalizing Russia, pushing it back into a geopolitical cage and transforming the countries on its border into bulwarks of US influence. Worse, as the months passed, Putin and his inner circle deceived themselves into believing that the US role in the

Ukrainian crisis was not only a threat to Russia's national security but an existential threat to the regime itself. During the February upheaval in Kiev, official Washington's open support for the democratic opposition and then active role in helping to organize an alternative to the Yanukovych regime, they argued, turned out to be not simply an effort to fashion a pro-Western Ukrainian government but, as the crisis unfolded, part of a broader and more basic strategy directed at change within Russia. In October 2014, Nikolai Patrushev, the head of the National Security Council and a member of Putin's inner circle, charged that current US policy belonged to a long tradition tracing back to the Soviet period, when the United States schemed to find and exploit the Soviet Union's "weak point," its energy-dependent economy, and, by manipulating oil prices and forcing the country to spend on defense, sought to bring the system down (Patrushev, 2014). To the obvious question of why, with today's Russia, the United States would want to do the same, his response was: because Russia stood as the only obstacle to the US desire to control the resources and orientation of the vast, rich region opened by the collapse of the Soviet Union. Lavrov, a month later, repeated what by then had become the common explanation for the harsh sanctions regime orchestrated against Russia by the United States. The concept underlying "the use of coercive measures," he stressed in a speech to the Russian Council on Foreign and Defense policy, "unequivocally demonstrates" that the West "does not merely seek to change Russian policy (which in itself is illusory), but it seeks to change the regime – and practically nobody denies this" (Lavrov, 2014).

It was the venomous core of the larger apprehension – namely, that the United States had come to see regime change as the preferred method for achieving its core strategic objectives and had translated this into a formal strategy, with Russia now the active target. Most

Western observers, however critical they might be of US interventions, from Iraq to Syria or, for that matter, in Ukraine, would not for a moment attribute that level of design to them, and, therefore, the natural instinct was to assume that members of the Putin regime did not really believe what they said and said it only as part of the intense propaganda war being waged. Much of the evidence, however, suggests that Putin and his closest colleagues did believe it. During fall 2014, I spent seven weeks in Moscow and spoke with many senior analysts and a number of officials. Nearly all of them, whether partisans or critics of Putin's foreign policy, agreed that this image of US purpose had become conviction. From there they often then stressed how high the stakes were for Putin in the confrontation over Ukraine.

Indeed, by early 2015 senior officials in the Obama administration accepted as reality that Putin had come to see US policy in these viscerally hostile terms. Their reaction fortified the standoff into which the two countries were sinking. Because they not only acknowledged the grim view Putin had of US policy but concluded that he was incorrigibly locked into it, they saw little that could be done to alter it and, therefore, as long as he remained in power, little that the two countries could accomplish together. Putin, as Vice President Biden characterized him when speaking at the Brookings Institution in May 2015, is "a practical guy," capable of calculating when it was in Russia's interest to cooperate with the United States (as on the Iran nuclear issue and in dealing with the threat from ISIS) and ready to back down when the cost of pushing on exceeded the value of the prize (Biden, 2015a). But the vice president's basic explanation for the crisis in US–Russian relations placed exclusive blame on Putin's wayward course once he returned to the presidency in 2012. Progress had been achieved with President Medvedev, but that ended when Putin came back and "set Russia on a very different course" of "aggressive repression at home" and "contempt for the sovereignty and territorial integrity of Russia's neighbors." In a phrase, the impasse was over Russia's "actions to weaken and undermine its European neighbors and reassert its hegemonic ambitions."

As for the Ukrainian crisis itself, nothing suggested that the September 2014 Minsk II Agreement had much chance of doing more than place shaky limits on the ongoing violence in eastern Ukraine. In May 2015, separatist leaders announced that the Novorossiya Project was a reach too far, and there were signs that Moscow saw little to be gained by a resumption of the war, although this offered no guarantee that it would not reignite. But Putin was obviously committed to shoring up the separatist regimes in their rump portion of the Donetsk and Lugansk provinces, and he had armed them to the point that, as one Baltic defense official said, they had militaries superior to some NATO countries. And neither Kiev nor the separatist leaders were about to do what the Minsk agreement required to achieve a political settlement. Nor were Russia or the United States and Europe prepared to insist on the compromises the warring parties needed to make to reach such a settlement, since their preoccupation remained the actions and aims of the other outside power(s). Instead, the war-ravaged separatist territories appeared to be turning into Europe's latest and most dangerous "protracted conflict," joining Transnistria, Nagorno-Karabakh, Abkhazia, and South Ossetia in the ring of instability now encircling Russia. Thus, the United States and Russia entered the second anniversary of the Donbas war utterly uncertain over what the future held and more deeply wedged in their new Cold War than ever before.

4

Where To?

Cold wars are not short-lived affairs. The original Cold War lasted, even if one assumes it ended before the Soviet Union collapsed, at least thirty-nine years. The Cold War between the United States and Iran began in 1979, and it continues thirty-six years later. In theory, if US and Russian leaders made it a conscious priority, they could, as might be hoped, make the new Cold War as short and shallow as possible. But neither side is thinking in those terms. If a cold war passes through stages, the United States and Russia are still in its early stages.

Even if it seems close to fantasy to expect either country to shift emphasis and make confining, let alone terminating, the new Cold War its first priority, are there no other ways by which the current confrontation might weaken? Might events let some of the air out of the current tension? Might the gauntlet laid down by the Islamic State be that event? Conceivably so – but even if the two countries find ways to cooperate in the war against the Islamic State, this will not automatically ease the tension at the base of the relationship – not unless both sides make that the larger objective. Even before the bloodshed in Paris, the downed Russian aircraft over Sharm el-Sheik, and the near simultaneous Beirut attack transformed what until then had been a local nightmare into a transcendent global threat, the two sides had moved closer together. In the diplomacy over Syria, conscious that waging one war required ending the other, they had agreed on which outsiders – including Iran – should be part of the negotiating process as well as on principles to guide a political settlement. They seemed likely to find a way to bring Syrian leadership and some part of the opposition to the table and to achieve at least a partial ceasefire. And the chances that the next phase of talks in the first half of 2016 would produce some kind of transitional Syrian government seemed relatively good. Even earlier the United States and Russia had agreed to cooperate on measures preventing dangerous incidents between their two air forces operating in Syrian air space.

None of this guaranteed that a political settlement could be reached in Syria or the civil war ended. US–Russian cooperation, even were it to deepen, cannot be expected to tame the swirling maelstrom of contending forces in and outside the country. Indeed, it was more likely that the maelstrom would constantly threaten to erode US–Russian cooperation. Similarly, while it might be hoped that a converging US–Russian struggle against the Islamic State would have a positive impact on the US–Russian standoff over Ukraine, the ongoing tensions in Ukraine were as likely to dilute the effects of this cooperation. Possibly Putin would view the effort against the Islamic State as cover for yielding to the urgency of easing Russia's economic plight and strike a more constructive stance in Ukraine. (The fear in some Western quarters that, on the other hand, Putin would try to use Russia's assistance in the fight against IS terror to extract Western concessions on Ukraine was not unreasonable; that he would succeed was.) As, if not more likely, however, the burden of Ukraine's unresolved crisis, with the ever present prospect that things could go awry and the crisis deepen, threatened not only to set limits on US–Russian cooperation but to reverse it.

Imagining that the IS threat had opened the way to an early end to the bitter animosity in US–Russian relations, therefore, was a leap too far. It underestimated how profound the gulf dividing the two countries had become. Reversing this state of affairs would not come easy. Nor would it happen on its own. The mutual mistrust and hostility that had hardened in the course of the Ukrainian crisis would not release its grip unless leadership on both sides chose to deal directly with its corrosive effect – unless they convinced themselves that letting events take their course would not be enough, that ending their new Cold War could only be by concerted effort.

Before something more fundamental can alter this reality, three things appear necessary: first, the emergence on both sides of a clearer sense of why it matters – why it is important for the United States and Russia to reintegrate their approach to current challenges, including the crisis in Ukraine, into the larger stakes each has in the relationship. Second, before either can begin designing a policy that effects that reintegration, each needs to pause for a moment and contemplate what part it played in producing the train wreck. Even if that is only internal to the policymaking process or perhaps only a shift in mental framework and not formally assessed, it is needed, first, to avoid repeating earlier mistakes and, second, where possible, to reverse their effects. And then, third, each government needs to plan policy within a wider compass. Rather than confining policy to the day's immediate problems, defined in narrow terms and addressed tactically, Russia and the United States need to set these problems – indisputably serious and requiring an effective response – in the larger context of where they want the US–Russian relationship to be several years down the road and how they might reconcile short-term imperatives with these longer-term objectives.

The Stakes

Most Americans would agree that it is not in US national interest for Russia to assume that it has the option of controlling political outcomes on its European borders, including in the new "lands in between," either by stirring political instability within them or by the direct or indirect use of force, although they would disagree over how far the United States should go in trying to deny Russia that option. Most Russians would agree that it is not in Russian national interest for the United States and any of its NATO allies to assume that they have the right to fashion arrangements on Russia's borders hostile to Russian interests, even if Russia's neighbors want such, although they would disagree over precisely what those interests are.

Presumably, however, most Americans and Russians would also not want to see Russia alienated from the West and persuaded that its only strategic option is with the rising powers of China, India, and Brazil – or, worse, only with countries equally alienated from the West. Presumably, even less would most Americans and a sizable portion of Russians wish to see Russia, in its alienation, committed to blocking and, wherever possible, damaging key US foreign policy initiatives. And presumably most Russians and Americans have no desire to see resurrected the Cold War military confrontation in Central Europe, let alone in circumstances that constantly teeter on the edge of exploding.

The challenge facing policymakers in both countries, therefore, is formidable. Designing policy that simultaneously strives to avoid outcomes that neither wants on two different levels and in two different time frames is no small task. It requires integrating short-term imperatives with the pursuit of long-term objectives, and that poses difficult analytical and political challenges that most governments, including those in the United States and Russia, rarely rise to meet – not, at least, on the scale needed to succeed. The reasons are many: from the tyranny of pressing events to the tension between the best ways of dealing with short-run problems while pursuing long-range goals; from the limited capacity of governments to do long-range strategic planning to the difficulty of achieving consensus on what by nature are remote objectives. And overcoming them has a chance only if key actors, beginning with national leaders, have the will to do so. Will of this intensity can come only from a conviction that the pain and ardor are worth it - which brings us back to how US and Russian leaders frame their stakes in the relationship.

If the stakes are confined to what in the other side's immediate behavior is preoccupying, they will be too low. They may well be urgent and vital to address, but they will provide no basis for either side to change the current course of US–Russian relations, no basis for designing an agenda appropriate to the larger challenges that each country faces, and no basis for averting the risks run and price paid for an ongoing cold war. Only if both sides - with the stress on both - step back from the moment's preoccupations, enlarge the narratives guiding current policy, and weigh seriously how to meet the challenges of the day without destroying a better future will they begin to pull themselves from the deep morass into which they have sunk.

The larger perspective needed is likely to have two components: first, a recognition of what is being lost as a result of the way each side struggles to counter the actions of the other and, second, a more urgent sense of large looming problems that will go unaddressed as long as the confrontation continues. In terms of what is being lost, start with the mantra of every US administration from Bush senior to Obama: a US desire to see Russia integrated into and benefiting from a prospering global economy. Banishing Russia from the G-8, suspending discussion of its inclusion in the OECD, isolating it within the G-20, and cutting links between key economic sectors moves in the opposite direction. Rather than nurture the large potential benefit of aligning a Russian economy rich in human and natural resources – and, until the 2015 recession, Europe's largest consumer market – with the wealth of North America and Europe, the two sides are pulling apart. In June 2015, at Russia's Council on Foreign and Defense Policy (SVOP), convened to discuss the economic implications of Russia's shifting geostrategic orientation, Andrey Klepach, the liberal former deputy minister of economic development, portrayed Russia's long effort to make itself a part of Europe's economic world as in crisis. Despite what will remain for some time extensive trade ties between Russia and Europe, the goal, he and others at the meeting stressed, was now fading (Zamyatin, 2015). Igor Ivanov, the former Russian foreign minister (1998–2004) and long an advocate of Euro-Atlantic cooperation, put it more dramatically in a speech in Riga three months later: "This continental rift, the parting of two European geopolitical plates, will exert a massive and long-term influence both on Europe and the world" (Ivanov, 2015).

Second, even before the Ukrainian crisis, Russia had begun rebelling against current arrangements within the International Monetary Fund (IMF) and other international financial institutions as well as against the position held by the dollar. For the United States and its European allies, economic sanctions have become the crucial mechanism by which to punish Russia for its aggression in Ukraine and to force a change in Russian behavior. Punishment they have been; a source of changed Russian behavior they have not, and whether they may yet be remains an open question. In addition, however, they carry further implications not only for Russia but also for China and other countries that could imagine themselves the target of what will look to them more like economic warfare than economic statecraft. The effort of the BRICS to create a set of institutions parallel to the IMF, the World Bank, and other development banks has barely begun and may never go far, or, if it does, may end by complementing the efforts of the dominant international financial institutions (IFIs). However, it is not clear that, when Washington and Brussels instantly reached for sanctions as the best means for addressing a Russian threat, they had weighed alternative strategies or, still more doubtful, had considered the incentive they were creating in Moscow and Beijing to create institutions competing with, rather than complementing, the institutions that have been the cornerstone of the international economic order.

Third, as noted in chapter 1, the web of arm control arrangements that reduced the number of nuclear weapons from 70,000 to 16,300 worldwide; ended a US–Russian race between offensive and defensive strategic nuclear programs; eliminated whole categories of nuclear weapons in US and Russian arsenals; secured nuclear weapons and materials in the former Soviet Union; constrained the spread of weapons of mass destruction; and placed limits on large standing armies in Europe while introducing transparency and mutual-trust-building measures into their operations – crumbling before – is now in danger of collapsing entirely.[1] Neither the United States nor Russia can alone or together fully restore this complex set of arrangements. But only if they re-engage can key elements in this architecture be saved, and that will not happen as long as the current standoff continues.

Fourth, Russia's energy relationship with the United States' European partners had been abrasive and troubled long before the Ukrainian crisis erupted – marked by Russian cutoffs in gas deliveries, tension over new pipeline routes, and frictions over the EU's "third energy package." In the wreckage over Ukraine, all sides, however, have vastly intensified their efforts to eliminate or circumvent vulnerabilities in a sphere equally vital to Europe and Russia: Russia by routing pipeline around Ukraine and emphasizing the development of its Asian market; Europe by stressing alternative sources of supply and fuels, shared resources, and backup strategies. As Biden put it in his Brookings speech, "When it comes to energy we need to work across the Atlantic to deny Russia the ability to use resources as a political weapon against their [sic] neighbors" (Biden, 2015a). The idea of collective, rather than competitive, energy security – of struggling to find mutually acceptable solutions to the problems plaguing Russia's oil and gas trade with Europe – lies buried under the debris of the new Cold War.

Fifth, the progress achieved in many of the twenty working groups under the US–Russia Bilateral Presidential Commission (BPC) has come to a halt. The agricultural working group had been coordinating efforts in food security, veterinary science, and domestic nutrition and had begun research on diseases in aquaculture, sustainable agricultural technologies, and forest regeneration. The science and technology group, in addition to focusing on nanotechnology, including nanotoxicology, had begun cooperating on climate change and streamflow monitoring as well as means for assessing the risk of extreme geophysical events. The health working group, beyond joint efforts to prevent and cure HIV/AIDS, was developing programs in the neurosciences, mental health, cancer, and bioimaging/bioengineering. The anti-narcotics working group had begun exchanging data on global drug flows, comparing effective drug treatment and rehabilitation programs and cooperating on countermeasures against drug money laundering. The military cooperation working group from 2010 to 2012 had organized more than forty coordinated undertakings, from naval discussions on the Asia–Pacific "rebalance" and operations in the Arctic to modeling military police reform in Russia after that in the United States, arranging military academy cadet exchanges, and carrying out search and rescue drills at sea, anti-piracy actions, and military security operations. All of this and a comparable range of practical activity in the emergency situations, counterterrorism, rule of law, cyber, innovation, education, and business development – not to mention the arms control – working groups have been "temporarily suspended," as the official US announcement puts it. Only activity under the space cooperation working group continues, and in May 2014 Russia's deputy prime minister, Dmitry Rogozin, indicated that Russia was unlikely to continue cooperating with the United States on the International Space Station after 2020.

Sixth, the likelihood that the political backsliding within Russia that has contributed significantly to the souring of US–Russian relations will soon turn in a more positive direction steadily recedes with each new round of accusations and demands. Important Russian voices, such as that of Alexei Kudrin, a trusted Putin advisor, and German Gref, the head of Russia's largest bank and a former minister of economic development, recognize that the absence of critical democratic institutions and genuine reform is stifling economic progress in Russia, and they are saying so. But the chance their urgings will gain traction, as history testifies, is far less likely the greater the tension in Russia's relations with the United States and Europe. The last time Russian leaders chose to lighten the heavy hand and let fresh air into the system occurred under Gorbachev, when tensions were easing and the Cold War ending. The deeper that US–Russian relations slide into tense dysfunction, the more the threat outside becomes the rationale for repressive measures, such as the foreign agents act and its sister component on "undesirable organizations." Under the BPC, the rule of law working group had begun focusing on a range of issues from prison reform to legal education, from the service of process under the Hague convention to probation and alternatives to incarceration – all now canceled.

As Russian and US leaders assess their current policy toward one another, sharpening objectives and measuring success, a full accounting ought not to overlook these six sizable losses. The ledger should also include the large looming problems that they will not be addressing – at least not effectively, and in most cases not at all. European security is the first of these. What seemed at hand with the end of the Cold War – a European continent, if not quite whole, then at peace – is no longer the case. Russia is again conducting military exercises, such as the one in May 2015, with nuclear-capable Iskander missiles and TU-22M3 aircraft forward-deployed into Kaliningrad and Crimea as well as SLBM-armed nuclear submarines put to sea under protective escort. NATO has announced a doubling in the size of its Rapid Reaction Force for Eastern European contingencies and the forward deployment into the Baltic or Poland of heavy armament to service a brigade-size force. Both have vastly increased the number of military exercises they plan for 2015 – Russia, up to 4,000 – and these are in nearly all cases designed to engage the forces of the other. Leaders on both sides speak once more of the heightened danger of a direct military conflict on Europe's new central front.

Scarcely three years before things fell apart, Russian and US leaders joined other OSCE heads of state gathered in Astana, Kazakhstan, and "recommitted" themselves to "the vision of a free, democratic, common and indivisible Euro-Atlantic and Eurasian security community stretching from Vancouver to Vladivostok, rooted in agreed principles, shared commitments and common goals" (OSCE, 2010). To note that stunningly little had been done along these lines in the two decades before, while accurate, rather misses the point: It is precisely this failure that has led the two sides to the current deadlock, and, while nothing guaranteed that, had the Ukrainian crisis not interceded, they would have soon become serious about building the pan-European security community they so often exhorted, the new Cold War does guarantee that they will have no chance to try. Hence, even the intermediate steps that were within reach, such as strengthening the Vienna Document providing for notification of military activity in Europe and the monitoring of armaments or enhancing the OSCE's efforts to deal with the protracted conflicts in the region, politically no longer are.

The Arctic, untainted by the legacy of the Cold War, might have been an ideal building block in constructing a Euro-Atlantic security community. This vast new frontier offered the United States, Russia, and Arctic NATO members a chance to prove that they could collectively resolve competing claims to resources, address a region critical to climate change, cope with immense environmental challenges, protect native populations, and marry technology and financing on a scale needed to develop the region's hydrocarbon resources, while demonstrating how collective security in a key portion of the Euro-Atlantic region might be fashioned. Instead the agenda remains fragmented, and even those items where cooperation had begun, such as on search and rescue, cleanup after oil spills, and controls on black carbon and methane emissions, are likely to progress slowly or not at all. Cooperation in other areas, such as on environmental cleanup in the highly polluted Russian Arctic Zone, joint exploration and development of oil and gas fields, military-to-military cooperation, and most major scientific collaborations, has ended. Meanwhile, discussion of military security in the Arctic, opposed in the Arctic Council, has little prospect in a NATO–Russia Council that has shut its doors. Instead national defense initiatives that two years ago were designed to protect economic interests and passageways are rapidly becoming adjuncts to preparations and exercises for the confrontation on Europe's new central front.[2]

Nor will the United States and Russia be addressing the looming perils in what is now a new nuclear age. An arms control regime in trouble is one thing; the incapacity or unwillingness of the two nuclear superpowers to begin grappling with the dangers posed by this new era – dangers that are far more complex than those of the Cold War era – is quite another. Technology, geometry, and geopolitics are coming together in ways creating a much greater risk that in a political crisis nuclear weapons will be fired, and, short of that, of a resumption of nuclear arms races – this time in the plural. The United States and Russia, in modernizing all three legs of their nuclear triads, have reopened a potential competition between offensive and defensive systems and introduced new destabilizing technologies, such as conventionally armed strategic missiles theoretically capable of striking the other side's nuclear weapons, thus blurring the firebreak between conventional and nuclear warfare. They are no longer alone. Other duos, in highly volatile relationships, such as India and Pakistan, are pressing ahead with ambitious nuclear programs, aspects of which, such as Pakistan's extensive short-range missile buildup and doctrine for use, carry great risks. India's determination to build the world's third triad of nuclear delivery vehicles, including advanced generation MIRVed ICBMs, means the country is moving beyond minimum deterrence. It and China, whose own programs are advancing in all of these categories, are headed for a strategic arms competition. This in turn will create an enormously complicated trilateral India–Pakistan–China nuclear relationship, which will in turn intersect with a potentially fraught Russia–US–China nuclear triangle. Superimposed on this maze are trends, including warfare's new cyber front, threatening traditional notions of nuclear deterrence and creating dangerous ambiguities over conventional military actions that could be read as a prelude to a nuclear attack.

In this new world of multiple advanced nuclear players – a world whose emerging dangers have scarcely been noticed and certainly not articulated – US and Russian leadership is badly needed, but alone not sufficient. In the new era, leadership in creating rules and limitations will have to come from a triumvirate of Russia, the United States, and China, but without the United States and Russia taking the lead it will not happen.[3] To the mounting but neglected hazards of the new nuclear age, one can add other realms where US–Russian–Chinese collaboration is essential but foreclosed by the Cold War between the United States and Russia, such as real progress in addressing climate change, containing the threat to global welfare from the flow of drugs, disease, arms, trafficked humans, counterfeit goods, including pharmaceuticals, and endangered species, and managing the increasingly vital security challenges in Northeast Asia.

The Path Not Taken

Imagining a path that will put the two countries back on track, limit the damage done by the current confrontation, and at least open the possibility of their collaboration in addressing the global challenges requiring their leadership is difficult. It is doubly difficult because the domestic political setting in both countries stands in the way. On both sides the media and much of the political elite are stuck inside the new Cold War and busy waging it. In the United States the political opposition would treat a more balanced and broad-visioned policy toward Russia as accommodation and a dangerous retreat in the face of Russian aggression. In Russia the leadership has spawned an anti-American fever that makes a dispassionate, open-minded discussion of policy toward the United States nearly impossible. Even when talk began of the United States and Russia coming together to battle the Islamic State, the thick crust of distrust evident in the ill intentions assigned by most in each country to the other remained undisturbed.

This makes it all the more important that US and Russian leaders, as they go about dealing with their immediate concerns, including the Ukrainian crisis, raise their eyes and reckon with the larger stakes that their countries have in the relationship. But this is only one essential part. In integrating short-term imperatives with long-term goals, it is equally important that both pieces be carefully calibrated, and that each be practical and designed for optimal effect. To make that possible, both sides need to face honestly where in the past policy fell short – where what could have been done differently offers insight into what might yet be done better. This is not to fix blame, which may have political utility back home but none in the bilateral relationship; rather, it is to uncover useful lessons.

US policymakers, for example, could ask themselves how the legitimate security concerns of the Central Europeans and Baltic states might have been addressed without expanding NATO, and Russian policymakers how Russia might have acted to make that everyone's preferred outcome. When in 2008 President Medvedev came forward with a multidimensional plan to enhance European security, would the United States and its NATO allies not have been wiser to try to refine it, rather than brushing it aside? After 2010, when Russia and NATO members began negotiating on missile defense cooperation, would the Russians not have been wiser to shape the system from inside, rather than insisting, in advance, on legal guarantees that the system not be directed against them?

Each might also ask how they could have acted differently to make Ukraine, as the eminent US diplomat Thomas Pickering (2015) now urges, "a bridge" between Europe's two halves, rather than an arena of competition. What difference might it have made if the United States had actively encouraged key states within the EU to think longer and harder about ensuring that the integration projects in Europe's two halves were complementary rather than competing?[4] And if Russia had chosen to give the EU the benefit of the doubt and engaged with it on the Eastern Partnership, rather than automatically casting it as a menace to Russia's interests? Or if, more recently, the United States had thought to share with Russia ideas on how its key projects in Europe and Asia-Pacific – the Transatlantic Trade and Investment Partnership and the Trans-Pacific Partnership – could accommodate Russia, rather than treating it as irrelevant? And had Russia chosen to encourage and complement US efforts to safely integrate a rising China into a swiftly changing international environment, rather than using its policy toward China as a counterbalance to aspects of US policy that it dislikes.

So might the effects have been different had the United States taken more seriously Russian concerns before intervening in Iraq, Libya, and Syria as well as their objections to the way the interventions were conducted. And, just as importantly, had Russia worked out an alternative approach to the serious problems presented by Saddam's Iraq, Gaddafi's Libya, and, in particular, Assad's Syria and been prepared to put its muscle and resources behind it, rather than simply opposing US actions.

Each of these choices was not obvious in its time, and the context of which each was a part would not have made any of them easy, but they were choices and, historians will say, not at all merely theoretical ones. Other choices were less grand, but they too, in small and large ways, figured in the untoward turns the US–Russian relationship took over these years. In 2008, when Russia went to war with Georgia, it could argue that the reckless gamble by the Georgian leader Mikheil Saakashvili in attacking Tskhinvali started it, but it would be hard pressed to justify expanding the war to Abkhazia and, least of all, then recognizing these two torn parts of Georgia as independent states. By this last step, Russia, to the consternation of even its closest allies, fed the impression that the Putin leadership would by means legitimate or not forcibly impose on neighbors the outcomes it wanted. In 2001, when the Bush administration unilaterally abrogated the ABM treaty, it had an understandable concern over rising nuclear threats, but by acting alone and over Russian objection, rather than first attempting to fashion a joint US–Russian response to third-party nuclear threats, it opened the way to what became a highly corrosive source of tension in US–Russian relations, one that may yet foster a renewed nuclear competition between offense and defense.

When in 2007, Putin, out of whatever level of frustration, decided to publicly and shrilly assail US foreign policy at the Munich Security Conference, a more constructive option would have been to bend every effort to make the strategic dialogue that the two sides had begun in 2003 work. This high-level, behind-the-scenes, well-designed forum offered the Russians the opportunity to engage the Bush administration on, rather than pillory it for, the things rankling them. Instead, Moscow contributed to the dialogue's short life by treating its representation carelessly, eventually putting it in the hands of a diplomat who the US side knew had no access to the top. During the Clinton administration, senior officials, as Strobe Talbott reports, thought of moments when they forced an issue with Yeltsin and his people as simply making them "eat their spinach" (Talbott, 2002). It reflected unconsciously the often imperious attitude that Americans and Europeans brought to the relationship. Rodric Braithwaite, the former British ambassador to the Soviet Union and Russia, reflecting on what he recognizes was "well meant," writes:

so for a decade Westerners lectured Moscow on where its real interests lay, and expected it to follow where the West led.

They rarely listened to what Russians said in response, because Russian concerns seemed unimportant, misguided, or unacceptable. The implication was that Russia, shorn of power, had no choice but to adopt "Western" values and become part of the "West." (Braithwaite, 2015)

If US and Russian policymakers want to draw insights from the past, there are other examples, but the most fateful of these are also the most recent – two in particular. In the Ukrainian crisis it may be, as many in the West assume, that Putin's Russia was simply waiting for a chance to rip Crimea from Ukraine. But, if, as is more likely, decisions were taken with strategic objectives in mind, annexation was a historic mistake. A Crimea with its dominant Russian population in revolt against the center and backed by Russian military force would have provided Moscow with leverage in the fluid tumult of Ukrainian politics. Annexation destroyed that leverage and transformed the crisis qualitatively, including its US–Russian dimension. Russia then compounded the error by mistakenly assuming that, in stoking separatism in eastern Ukraine, it would have still greater purchase over political outcomes in the country. Instead, while unquestionably greatly burdening Ukraine's central government, Russia has made Ukraine into a uniformly hostile neighbor, created an irredentist grudge that will haunt the relationship for years, and tied itself to separatist elements neither entirely under its control nor entirely legitimate in the eyes of the people they govern.

Earlier in the crisis, the United States and the Europeans almost certainly erred by capitulating to the rush of events and too hastily walking away from the arrangement the French, German, and Polish foreign ministers had worked out with the Yanukovych government. Even when Yanukovych fled, it should have been possible to construct an interim government of national unity that preserved a meaningful voice for the eastern provinces. The arrangement improvised by a Ukrainian parliament in chaos was guaranteed to seal the polarization of the country and create the opening that Donetsk and Lugansk separatists seized two months later, although, it should be added, it provided no legitimate excuse for Russia to intrude in the conflict with military force.

A Path Forward

There is no path forward unless the two countries travel it together. They arrived here together and only together can they alter the relationship's currently unhappy trajectory. One side can take the lead, as the Obama administration did in launching the reset, but the other side will have to quickly follow. Admittedly, as said earlier, all of this rests on an assumption that many in the West would reject. No basis exists, they would argue, for assuming that Putin's Russia would do its part. If one believes, as many do, that Russian policy is driven by the character of the regime and not by the interaction with others, then it would be foolish – indeed, dangerous – to expect Putin and those around him to respond constructively to an extended US hand. They, critics would have it, are driven to do what they do by what is required to keep them in power. Defining the stakes as I have and assuming that the Russians would ever see them as such, let alone allow them to shape their behavior, is simply illusory.

Perhaps so. There is no obvious way to prove this perspective wrong other than to test it. Testing it, however, should not be thought of as particularly parlous. Given the United States' overwhelming economic, military, and strategic advantage, it can afford to explore possibilities, and, if it turns out that Putin's Russia is as unredeemable as critics insist, the US has the time and wherewithal to shift course. For Russia's immediate neighbors, and about whom Washington should care, the same is not true. But even in this case the still larger advantage that Europe in league with the United States has over Russia gives the West the upper hand were Russia to pose a direct threat beyond the trouble that it is capable of creating on its border. Dealing effectively with that capability is important, but it is not a reason to reject the gamble that, approached skillfully, the Putin government can be drawn into a constructive interaction that begins to lead out of the current impasse.

Again, however, the process has no chance if one side's initiative is not swiftly reciprocated by the other. For change of this kind to gather any momentum, two things would appear necessary. First, each side needs to suspend the premise presently guiding its approach to the other. The Russian side needs to entertain the possibility that the United States is not bent on undermining Russia's national security and even the regime itself. The US side needs to consider the possibility that what it sees as implacable in Russia's behavior is not and what it fears in Russia's aims may be misplaced. One should not expect the impossible: neither leadership will casually toss aside views that have slowly formed and by now are deeply rooted. Rather it is to suggest that, if they wish to test the possibility of rebuilding the relationship – this time on sturdier ground than before – they must first be willing to challenge their working premises.

Doing so requires no change in policy and, in fact, by itself proves nothing. It simply creates a basis for testing. The need to cooperate in the war against the Islamic State may form a test. Cooperation will at points require trusting the other side, and if the actions of each justify that trust, a building block will have been created. Testing, however, almost certainly requires one of two further steps. The most natural – but least effective – of these is to take a small, low-cost initiative and see whether it is reciprocated. If it is, then proceed to the next. During the first Reagan administration the simple step that persuaded the president of Soviet openness to dealing was the release of seven Pentecostal Christians, who, blocked from emigrating, had been holed up in the US embassy for five years.[5] It would require no great act of imagination (or courage) either in Moscow or Washington to identify a small step that could serve this purpose. If this is the inferior approach, however, it is because small steps are difficult to manage in a way productive of a cumulative effect and, more importantly, because they do not get at the root of the problem.

The step that can, but that is rarely given a serious chance, is strategic dialogue, and in present circumstances it is a step that has no chance at all. Neither side sees any point in trying to engage in a serious discussion of the other side's concerns, desires, and expectations or to explain its own. Indeed, on the US side the very idea of dialogue – of talking to Putin's government in other than highly selective fashion – runs counter to its basic policy of isolating the Russian regime. When John Kerry, following his meetings with Putin and Lavrov in Sochi in May 2015, noted that it was "necessary to keep the lines of communication open between the US and Russia," saying that "there was no substitute for direct talks," folks back in Washington immediately walked his comment back (BBC, 2015). A former aide to Vice-President Biden called the Kerry initiative "counterproductive," forcing Obama to do "a little mopping up" in his forthcoming trip to Western Europe (Davis, 2015). In his 2015 Fourth of July greeting to Obama, Putin expressed confidence that, by "building a dialogue based on the principles of equality and mutual respect for each other's interests," the two countries are capable of "resolving the most complex international problems" and of coping with "global threats and challenges," but nothing suggested that he was ready for the give-and-take that a productive dialogue would require (Putin, 2015).

In any event, dialogue or a readiness to talk to one another is not the same thing as strategic dialogue. Although the term appears in different contexts, such as the regular meetings between foreign and economic ministers in the US–China Strategic and Economic Dialogue, the US–India Strategic Dialogue among cabinet-level officials, or the problem-solving relationship that Strobe Talbott had with a counterpart from the Russian Ministry of Foreign Affairs, Georgy Mamedov, during the Clinton administration, none of these examples fits in this instance. Rather, the two sides need to find a way to lower their guard and have a deep probing exploration of what lies at the base of their badly damaged relationship. The closest model is the US–Russia strategic dialogue organized soon after the US invasion of Iraq in 2003.

In spring 2003, with the relationship fraying in the wake of the US invasion of Iraq, the two leaderships decided to organize a high-level strategic dialogue freed from normal bureaucratic procedures and conducted by senior officials close to Putin and Bush. They assigned it four tasks: to elaborate the content of the strategic partnership that the two presidents had earlier embraced, identifying areas of cooperation and setting out a framework for policymaking; to monitor implementation of agreed policies and identify log-jams that should be raised to the presidential level for resolution; to create a venue within which sensitive issues could be discussed candidly and in confidence; and to identify areas of competition and ways of reducing their effects.

Conducted at the level of senior advisors to the presidents, the dialogue met once a month, alternating between Washington and Moscow. They agreed on each meeting's agenda in advance, but with the understanding that the entire range of issues, including the most sensitive, such as developments in the post-Soviet space, would be covered. At the outset they also adopted a one-page set of principles to guide their work, containing a promise of no surprises, no zero-sum thinking, and no reporting to third countries, and that each would raise concerns in private channels before going public. Early in the process they also developed what they called the presidential "checklist" – a set of concrete tasks assigned to specific agencies that were to report back on their progress at regular intervals, progress that would be reviewed by the presidents at summit meetings.

The dialogue continued into 2004, when, having gone through a series of personnel changes on the Russian side removing it from Putin's close involvement, the Bush administration lost interest. The experience also held other negative lessons, such as the capacity of bureaucracies on both sides to frustrate the checklist process if not carefully disciplined, but these lessons are less relevant to the strategic dialogue needed now, because, as a function of the new US–Russia Cold War, when nearly all ties are severed, a government-to-government engagement of this kind appears out of the question.

A strategic dialogue would have to be informal, conducted by senior figures out of government but with the trust and blessing of the two presidents.[6] In ways not open to senior officials, they would have to be free to probe as frankly as possible the rawest subjects and carry as far as possible thoughts on where and how the two governments might find common ground. They would neither represent official policy nor be taxed with justifying it. Their whole purpose would be to conceive an alternative path for US–Russian relations, demonstrate its feasibility, and step by step bring the results to the two presidents and their senior advisors. National leaders would then need to decide whether they were prepared, if only tentatively, to move in this direction.

Reconciling Current Imperatives with Longer-Term Goals

When and if either or both leaderships think it wise and safe – or, indeed, imperative – to alter course, the challenge will be to integrate the pursuit of immediate policy objectives into a larger framework preserving long-term goals. How – each government needs to ask itself – can we best deal with today's urgent challenges in ways that facilitate, rather than impede, the future relationship we want?

Doing this well requires reversing the usual policy planning process: rather than starting with the challenges of the moment, designing a strategy to deal with them, and using this as the framework for defining longer-term goals, Russian and US policy planners would do better by beginning at the other end, developing a realistic strategic vision for the out years, and working back. In an ideal world they would do this together, allowing the process in one country to intersect with and shape the other. But there is nothing ideal about the moment, and the most one might expect is an uneven, halting process where the efforts of one side may encourage the other to move along the same path.

Each would start by envisaging the US–Russian relationship that it wished to see a decade from now and a realistic set of goals underpinning it. Next each would develop less ambitious, intermediate objectives that over the next five years would begin moving the relationship toward this longer-term set of goals. And, finally, each would re-examine current policy to see in what ways it should be adjusted to promote these intermediate objectives without jeopardizing the achievement of vital short-term objectives. Implementing policy, however, would unfold in reverse. Optimizing each country's approach to the issues on its immediate agenda would open the way to attack a larger set of intermediate objectives, and progress on them, if to the benefit of each, would, in turn, put the two countries on a path bring-ing them closer to what is compatible in their strategic visions.

The function of a strategic vision is to serve as a working hypoth-esis and a lodestar, giving policy a sustainable framework, a coherent set of aims, and criteria for measuring success. Coming full circle, it should be the creature of the fundamental stakes the two countries have in the relationship. In this case, it should feature, as the two have often said, "a Europe whole, free, and at peace"; progress toward something of the same in a rapidly changing Asia-Pacific, including promoting the peaceful rise of China; initial steps toward reducing the dangers that the new multipolar nuclear age poses; and a modus viv-endi permitting a constructive interaction between the United States and Russia aimed at stable change and mutual security in and around Eurasia.

If these seem lofty and impractical goals, it is a measure of how thoroughly the new US–Russia Cold War has altered earlier perspec-tives. Scarcely two years before the Ukrainian crisis erupted, a group of former senior government officials and business leaders from North America, Europe, and Russia, after working on the issue for two years, thought it not too late to urge "building an inclusive, undivided, func-tioning Euro-Atlantic Security Community" – a community "without barriers, in which all would expect resolution of disputes exclusively by diplomatic, legal, or other nonviolent means, without recourse to military force or the threat of its use."[7] They added that, within this community, governments "would share a common strategy and understanding in the face of common threats" and accept that the "most efficient way to tackle threats, both internal and external, is through cooperation" (EASI, 2012).

The group fully appreciated the obstacles standing in the way, for, as they said, "Old twentieth-century divisions along with unresolved post-Cold War security issues and patterns of thinking rooted in confrontation perpetuate mistrust and division within the region and leave its nations and societies dangerously ill-prepared to handle the challenges of the twenty-first century." But ten years from now, as they argued then, the "historical enmities between Russia and the United States and among others across the region" that prevented "effective cooperation in meeting urgent security challenges, such as the risk of renewed violence raised by unresolved conflicts between and within Euro-Atlantic states," will, if left to fester, be still more dangerous. So will "the threat of cyberwar and the tensions generated over the critical trade in gas." And no price will be higher than the one they saw in 2012: that "the lack of Euro-Atlantic unity" will prevent "governments and leaders from providing the global leadership so essential in a stressed and increasingly fragmented international order."

"Launching and advancing this process," they recognized, depended "on identifying a few critical areas where progress would break the current inertia and give the idea of building a Euro-Atlantic Security Community tangible form," and they suggested a number of intermediate objectives with this in mind. To end the paralysis surrounding the protracted conflicts in Azerbaijan, Georgia, and Moldova, they recommended, among other things, a stronger role for the OSCE, allowing it to develop direct links to civil society, to better integrate traditional and Track II diplomacy, and to employ "assemblies of elders," as Nelson Mandela did in South Africa, to cut through critical bottlenecks. To deal with historically fraught relationships, such as between Russia and the Baltic states, Turkey and Armenia, and Armenia and Azerbaijan, the Commission offered the specific lessons learned in the historical reconciliation effort undertaken by Poland and Russia. To enhance energy security, the group urged Russia and the European Union to establish a joint Center for Energy Efficiency drawing in countries from the entire Euro-Atlantic region, as well as steps to strengthen an existing early warning mechanism for potential gas supply disruptions "by undertaking mutual obligations and a detailed backup plan." Add to this the Arctic and the opportunity there to prove graphically how a Euro-Atlantic security community might work.

In what today seems a wistful plea, a primary objective should be, the group argued, "to transform and demilitarize strategic relations between the United States/NATO and Russia." What the Commission recommended, however, was practical and feasible. It was also central to any hope of strengthening the military dimension of European security. With trends again moving in the opposite direction it will be more so in the future. Far from "demilitarizing strategic relations between the United States/NATO and Russia," US defense officials by July 2015 were speaking of Russia as the "greatest security threat to the United States," or as General Joseph Dunford testified before Congress that month, "If you want to talk about a nation that could pose an existential threat to the United States, I'd have to point to Russia . . . If you look at their behavior, it's nothing short of alarming" (Lamothe, 2015). The new US National Military Strategy released that month, in sharp contrast to its previous version, described Russia as a state "attempting to revise key aspects of the international order" and one "acting in a manner that threatens our national security interests" (US Department of Defense, 2015). By summer 2015, the Pentagon had begun shifting funds within the defense budget to deal with what it saw as a growing Russian conventional and nuclear threat (Weisgerber, 2015). And Russia was following suit, issuing nuclear warnings, touting force modernization plans, and introducing a new naval doctrine with renewed emphasis on the Atlantic and Arctic expressly to deal an "increasing" NATO threat.

It cannot be in the interest of Russia, any of the NATO members, or the countries caught between to see the divide in Europe remilita-rized, safeguards dismantled, resources diverted to a military buildup, and armed forces once more poised for action against the other. An important part of a strategic vision for Russia, as for the United States, therefore, should be halting and reversing this trend. The urging of the Euro-Atlantic Security Initiative still holds, if and when both sides are ready to try. "Military leaders and defense officials" from the United States, NATO, and Russia, the group argued, "must be charged" by national leaderships "with engaging in a comprehensive and sustained dialogue that includes all aspects of the problem: perceptions, capa-bilities, operational doctrines, and intentions." The aim would be not negotiated treaties or a new security architecture – at least not yet – but, rather, a "dynamic confidence-building process."

In the conventional area, the focus of the dialogue ought to be on "transparency in deployments, limits on exercises near the NATO–Russian border, constraints on maneuvers and reinforcements" in sensitive regions, and the reduced forward deployment of desta-bilizing offensive weapons systems. Given the concern stirred by Russia's resort to what those in the West call "hybrid warfare" in the Ukrainian case, this too would need to be part of the dialogue. An intermediate step in the area of tactical nuclear weapons with a sta-bilizing effect would be separating warheads from delivery systems and "storing them some distance apart." And in the area of European missile defense, the hope would be that the sides could agree to share intelligence and jointly man operations centers "to eliminate the risk that either NATO or Russia would misread a decision to launch interceptors."

Finally, as others have suggested, forty years after East and West began deconstructing the original Cold War by signing the Helsinki Charter, Europe, its peace of mind and basic stability again disrupted, needs another Helsinki-like process – that is, another attempt to organize an active regional security dialogue aimed at finding some common understanding of how the peace and welfare of the continent are to be maintained (Rojansky, 2015; Stent, 2015). The lead could come from the Europeans (Germany will chair the OSCE in 2016), but, just as in the earlier case, Moscow and Washington's support and leadership will determine success or failure.

Second, common sense suggests that, ten years from now, US as well as Russian leaders would want the two countries working together to enhance security in Asia-Pacific and to ensure that the historic shifts taking place within the region occur peacefully. US–Russian cooperation, in lieu of competition – alas, the far more likely outcome – will come about, however, only if it is actively pursued. Equally obvious, any level of collaboration between the two would have to respect their key relationships with, in particular, China, but, in the US case, with Japan and South Korea as well. Indeed, the point of their cooperation would be to help make this complex matrix of relations more constructive and beneficial for all in the region.

In 2012 Thomas Graham, George W. Bush's senior Russia advisor, suggested that, if the two countries wanted to begin filling the void in their relationship created by the long-standing failure to develop a sense of "what of strategic significance they should do together for mutual benefit over the long term," Northeast Asia represented the least burdened opportunity to do so (Graham, 2012). Considering the mounting importance of the region for both countries, he argued, they had good reason to come together around two key objectives: first, developing Russia's vast region east of Lake Baikal through "a multilateral effort under Russia's guidance" with heavy US participation. It is, he insisted, in their mutual interest to reinforce "Russia's sovereignty over and its ability to manage effectively" this region, just as it is to see Russia with an economic base allowing it to contribute to the economic dynamism of the region, including a much expanded trade between Russia's Far East and the US Pacific Coast. As a natural second objective Graham proposed a US–Russia dialogue focused on how power shifts and security challenges in the region could be best managed. Because China is central in this picture, it too should be part of the dialogue, and, as Graham advised, at some point Japan and South Korea as well.

Nor may it be beyond imagining that the United States and Russia would both see an advantage in pushing to transform a forum such as the East Asia Summit into a prototype pointing toward a more institutionalized Asia-Pacific security community. Or in the same spirit, just as the United States seeks to develop the Trans-Pacific Trade Partnership in ways that attract Chinese participation rather than hostility and counter moves, Moscow and Washington might each envisage a process by which Russia also joins the TPP. As the two major powers that are not party to the explosive territorial disputes in the South and East China Seas, Russia and the United States could play the role of mediators, a role that would be considerably strengthened if they acted in tandem. So would their influence, if exercised together, be greater in defending open access to the region's vital sea lanes of communication.

Welcome as this vision may be in theory, not only is it not at hand, at the moment it is a receding prospect. Hence, each country would need to set intermediate objectives that put a brake on the negative momentum and begin edging the two in the other direction. Thus, for example, on the North Korean nuclear issue, Russia, rather than continuing to follow in the shadow of the Chinese lead, might well make it a priority to reconcile the US and Chinese approaches to the problem, and the United States might well attach the same importance to the

Russian role in the six-party talks as it did in the Iran negotiations. Or Russia might be invited to join the United States and China with a commitment to limit greenhouse gases and speed the development of alternative fuels comparable to theirs in the milestone US–China November 2014 agreement. This could not happen in time to influence the December 2015 Paris climate summit, but, were three of the world's four largest greenhouse gas emitters to set this example, it would be a powerful influence in the future. At a minimum, the United States needs to acknowledge Russia's potential role in the Asia-Pacific and factor the country into its vision for the region. Symptomatically, when Hillary Clinton delivered her October 2011 speech underscoring the United States' "pivot" to a region that she described as "a key driver of global politics," no mention was made of Russia (Clinton, 2011). For its part, Russia needs to move from mistrusting closer US–Chinese ties to weighing what it gains from a constructive, well-functioning relationship between the two most important global players.

The third dimension of a strategic vision is the most elusive and remote from US and Russian consciousness, but also potentially the most fateful. Were the two countries focused, as they should be, on the looming dangers in a new genuinely multipolar nuclear age, the need for their leadership in bringing order to the emerging disorder would be inescapable. They are the essential two countries in moving to a new generation of arms control that goes beyond numerical limitations and begins to contain the potentially destabilizing effects from the technological frontiers being crossed – from blurring the line between conventional and nuclear war with conventionally armed hypersonic missiles capable of counterforce (nuclear) missions to the deployment of weapons making space a lethal dimension of nuclear war. They, with China – and only the two of them together can persuade China to join them – are the sole states capable of shaping a multilateral framework that begins to deal with the immensely complicated but easily foreseeable perils of the emerging strategic nuclear triangles among India, Pakistan, and China and China, Russia, and the United States. And, if any chance exists that the highly destabilizing effects from integrating cyber-warfare into nuclear war can be mitigated, again, it can come about only through US, Russian, and Chinese cooperation.

That achieving any of this seems for now an utter flight of fancy ought not to be confused with what leaders in Moscow and Washington would want were they to think hard about where they wished the two countries to be ten years from now. In the meantime, the intermediate objectives they should set for themselves are obvious. Everything starts from the urgency of stemming the crumbling edifice of existing arms control arrangements. No US or Russian government, short of one in the hands of its most hawkish elements, can want to see the limits on unconstrained nuclear programs, the measures permitting each side to track the forces and activities of the other side, and the safeguards against the unintended use of a nuclear weapon vanish.

Surely each, therefore, should strive to save the now imperiled 1987 treaty eliminating US and Russian intermediate-range ballistic missiles (INF), not least because burying this treaty guarantees that dealing with the broader challenge of INF at the core of other countries' nuclear postures goes by the board. Similarly, before either country invests too heavily in missile defense, it is important that they get back to creating limits that avert the wasteful and dangerously destabilizing effects of an offense–defense competition, the folly of which US and Soviet leaders recognized four decades ago. For the moment, both countries are proceeding with reductions and inspections under the New START agreement, a vital piece whose loss would pull the last brick from the imperiled architecture. Furthermore, the frustrating but important task of reducing and controlling tactical nuclear weapons in Europe takes on vastly greater moment when both sides are modernizing these weapons, one side is re-emphasizing their role in war, and the risk that it could come to that is once more thinkable. Finally, an easy constructive step on Russia's part would be to reverse its decision not to attend the next Nuclear Security Conference that the United States will hold in spring 2016. This effort to secure nuclear materials around the world, as noted earlier, was one of the four critical objectives of the "reset" for the Obama administration, and Russia was a key participant in all of the earlier conferences.

No element in a strategic vision for either country, however, is more critical or vexed than the fourth. Almost from the beginning, signs indicated that Russia's painful adjustment to loss of empire would figure uneasily in US–Russian relations. Where the US–Soviet contestation had been direct and global during the Cold War, in the post-Cold War period its friction-generating counterpart would be indirect and regional. Always in the background, whatever else was on the US–Russian agenda, Moscow's heavy-handed treatment of its neighbors and the low-boil tensions over the US role in the region constantly gnawed at the relationship, finally culminating in the current crisis over Ukraine.

Central as a factor shaping US–Russian relations, although never central in the diplomacy between the two countries, the interaction between Russia and the United States in the post-Soviet space should figure prominently in any US or Russian strategic vision. This is so, first, because a sustainable US–Russian working relationship will not be possible until they have found a workable understanding on the role each is to play in what is the critical core of Eurasia and, second, because the Eurasian core merges with the three regions key to the evolution of the global setting: a now troubled European continent, the turbulent Islamic south, and a rising Asia-Pacific. For Russia and the United States, the reality is not so much that Halford McKinder and his contemporary admirers are correct in stressing that he who rules the Eurasian heartland will rule the world, but that the dynamics that rule within this heartland will dictate the character of world politics. The United States fought all of its post-1945 wars around the Eurasian core, and virtually every major menace that the United States will face over the next seventy years will originate there. For Russia it is its world. Therefore, scarcely any strategic, long-term goal can be more important for both countries than working together to promote stable change and mutual security in and around the Eurasian core.

It is the natural inclination of every major power both to assume that it is entitled to pride of place within its region and, when possible, to enforce it. This is historically true of the United States and will be of China and India in coming years. And so too is it of Russia. With others who have a stake in the region, the natural product is competition over cooperation, a result reinforced when issues are treated in piecemeal and disembodied fashion. Therefore, were the United States and Russia to make stable change and mutual security in and around the Eurasian core their long-term goal, it would be important, as an intermediate goal, for them to treat the threats to stability and those yet to come – from the uneasy peace on the Korean peninsula to the tinder on the Indian subcontinent, the threat posed by the Islamic State, the violence in the Caucasus, and, ultimately, the crisis in Ukraine – as of a piece. Obviously tying all of these challenges together would be too formidable, too large, and too elusive to constitute an active agenda. But it could begin to form a mindset, and this would have a positive effect on the things the two could do together.

For example, even before the Paris attacks both countries regarded the growing menace of the Islamic State as a threat to national security

– among senior Russian officials the principal threat; among US officials, one of the top three threats. Once the threat became global and it was obvious that the events in Paris could happen again in Moscow or Chicago, Moscow and Washington had compelling reason to reconcile their positions on the Syrian civil war and join forces against the Islamic State. As noted, in November in the Vienna negotiation they did edge toward agreement on steps intended to end the Syrian war and begin a political process. But the path to military cooperation in the other war remained littered with obstacles, many of them rooted in an instinctive mistrust of the other side's commitment to cooperation or, worse, ulterior motive for seeking it. Hence, manifestly important as is the need to halt the violence in Syria and roll back the Islamic State, the barriers to effective US–Russian cooperation remain. They would be more easily scaled were cooperation thought of not simply as a response to an urgent problem but as an intermediate step toward the larger goal. It surely offers a basis, if not for formal cooperation, then for parallel actions that complement each other's efforts. By September 2015 the two governments appeared to be edging toward at least testing the idea of working together to fight the Islamic State. The obstacle remained their sharply conflicting approaches to a political settlement of the Syrian civil war. Overcoming that divide seemed an all too obvious necessary objective for both. It would scarcely ensure an end to that awful conflict, but it would alter the role of the conflict in their relationship and make cooperation against the Islamic State possible. Similarly, rather than keeping their collective efforts at arm's length, they could focus more on how they might pool the resources of NATO, the Collective Security Treaty Organization (CSTO), and the Shanghai Cooperation Organization (SCO) to fight the scourge of narcotics flowing out of Afghanistan into Central Asia and on to Russia, China, and Europe, and, beyond that, to effect the broader cooperation that will be essential in coping with what is likely to be the ongoing – perhaps escalating – instability in Afghanistan and the wider region. Progress, even modest progress, toward these and a strategic vision's other goals, however, will remain frozen until the Ukrainian crisis – the ultimate collision between US–Russian interests in the post-Soviet space – fades or is surmounted.

Policy Here and Now

The final piece in the sequence, were Moscow and Washington to begin working their way out of the new Cold War, depends on how the two deal with the day's challenges – none more central than the confrontation over Ukraine. Being realistic, it is entirely possible that there is no solution in the Ukrainian case, and that what lies ahead is a frozen conflict, with shaky but relatively permanent limits to the violence. For the foreseeable future political realities in Kiev and the separatist strongholds, as well as in Washington and Moscow, make unlikely the compromises that will be necessary all around to break free of the impasse. The Minsk II agreement signed in September 2014 has twelve provisions, roughly half that address the violence, and the other half that provide partial steps toward a political settlement. All were to have been completed by the end of 2015. The measures to separate the warring parties, stand down forward-deployed heavy armament, exchange prisoners of war, and silence the guns, although regularly violated, nonetheless stand a chance of working, albeit imperfectly – if Russia and the United States with its European allies insist that the side they support make it work.

The odds favoring any one of the three critical elements in the agreement's other half, however, appear negligible at best. The agreement calls for local elections in the breakaway regions, elections that are to be free and according to Ukrainian law, elections that Kiev will insist produce leaders whom it regards as legitimate interlocutors; the separatist leaders appear to have no intention of allowing elections that would threaten their power. Second, and more difficult, the parties are mandated to decentralize political authority in Ukraine and grant the rump portions of the Donetsk and Lugansk provinces controlled by the separatists an unspecified degree of political autonomy. No Ukrainian government, as testified by the legislation passed by the Rada in summer 2015, is prepared to grant the near political independence demanded by the separatists, and the separatists, backed by Moscow, have no intention of accepting any arrangement that would make their territories again an integral part of Ukraine. Third, between local elections and constitutional reform permitting decentralization, Ukraine is to regain full control over its border with Russia, allowing it control over Moscow's supply lines to the separatist territories. Short of a political settlement satisfactory to Moscow, it seems safe to predict that Moscow will not abandon the access by which it sustains the separatist regimes.

Hence, the United States and Russia will both need to reframe the assumptions underpinning policy. Both have designed policy for a fluid – a dangerously fluid – crisis in which the objective is to frustrate what are assumed to be the aggressive aims of the other side. Ahead, however, the challenge is likely to be an immobile standoff, with neither the United States nor Russia upping the ante out of a preoccupation with threatening moves by the other side. This scarcely guarantees that events could not spin out of control largely independent of their actions. But it does mean that both governments are more likely to find themselves struggling to maintain their current positions: the United States with the immense and fraught effort to aid Ukraine dig out from the economic hole that it is in, while helping to train and equip a Ukrainian military capable of its own defense; Russia with maintaining politically suspect separatist regimes in isolated and economically devastated communities, while continuing to bear the costs of the West's punitive sanctions.

"Neither war nor peace" has been a Russian strategy before, stretching back to Leon Trotsky's misbegotten gambit in the February 1918 Brest–Litovsk negotiations with Germany as German armies marched across Russia's collapsed defenses. It was repeated over much of the Brezhnev era in the Soviet approach to the Arab–Israeli conflict. One wonders, however, whether it is the optimal Russian strategy for dealing with the Ukrainian crisis. Does it not make more sense to mediate a reconciliation between Ukraine's warring parts that protects Russia's interests in eastern Ukraine and reduces the white-hot hostility toward Russia in the rest of Ukraine? Rather than chase the illusion that it can engineer an independent enclave within Ukraine wielding a veto over the country's relationship with NATO and the EU, it would seem more in Russia's interest to shed the burden of subsidizing the country's division and strive for a Ukraine that is a bridge, rather than a moat, between Europe's two halves, provided that this left Ukraine out of NATO and a vibrant trading partner for Russia.

But it will not happen unless the United States also adjusts its policy. If the United States too wishes to optimize short-term policy compatible with a long-term strategic vision and begin edging away from the wreckage in US–Russian relations, it will need to shift course along three policy vectors. The first vector has been its answer to Russian aggression in Ukraine. The United States' primary instrument and easiest recourse has been sanctions. But sanctions, particularly when wielded with shifting and imprecise purpose, are both ineffective and a barrier to the pursuit of larger, longer-term goals. As punishment for

Russia's violation of a crucial Europe norm in seizing another country's territory, sanctions focused on Crimea fit the transgression and should be left in place. As a deterrent to further aggression or as leverage forcing Russia to reverse course, they are a blunt instrument of doubtful effectiveness if the criterion is not how much pain they cause but how much they change Russian behavior. Asymmetrical policy responses are by their nature weaker than responses in kind. The challenge posed by Russian actions in Ukraine has from the beginning been military in nature, and so should have been the US and European response.

De-escalating the Ukrainian crisis, therefore, ironically almost certainly requires moving from sanctions to shoring up Ukraine's military defenses – focusing on reducing Ukrainian vulnerability rather than counting on Russian vulnerability to solve the problem. The emphasis should be on reforming and training to a modern standard Ukraine's defense forces. As the capacity of those forces to use advanced arms increases, they should be supplied with those most effective against Russian capabilities. At the same time, the corollary to the Ukrainian crisis, the growing anxiety of Russia's newest NATO neighbors, needs to be addressed in the measured terms already begun by NATO.

The near-term risk, however, is that the Minsk ceasefire, tattered as it is, collapses entirely. In that case the United States and a number of European allies will almost surely feel compelled to supply the Ukrainian military with lethal aid, including anti-tank weapons, such as Javelin missiles, advanced radar systems, reconnaissance drones, and armored Humvees. In the heat of battle, and, more so, if in anticipation of such, these arms begin to flow, Russia will almost surely sharply escalate its own involvement. Then the slow, steady, stabilizing effect of efforts to create a defensible Ukraine will be swamped by the highly destabilizing effect of an unpredictable military confrontation.

Strengthening Ukrainian defenses and reassuring nervous NATO allies are, however, but half of what is needed, and, if the other half is missing, these steps will be escalatory, not de-escalatory – an impediment, rather than an aid on the path to reconciling short-term imperatives with long-term goals. This other half includes directly and explicitly conveying to Moscow everything the United States is doing and will do to address the military challenge that Russia raises, while also forcefully and convincingly offering the Russian leadership the option of moving in the opposite direction – of together building down.

A small step might be the suggestion of Fiona Hill and Stephen Pifer (2015) that, in order to minimize the danger of an explosive incident as the result of the harassing patrols that Russian air and sea craft are now conducting near NATO borders, military professionals from the two sides duplicate what their predecessors achieved during the Cold War in negotiating the 1972 Prevention of Incidents at Sea Agreement and the 1989 Dangerous Military Activities Agreement. Similarly, as analysts at the European Leadership Network recommend, NATO and Russia might sensibly release some of the tension over military activity in the center of Europe by warning in advance of exercises and ensuring that observers from the other side participate (Frear et al., 2015). However, unless linked to a larger agenda of potential measures intended to contain and stabilize the growing military confrontation on the Central European front, small steps of this kind are not likely to be given a chance. Nor, even if adopted, will they get at the core problem or turn a dimension deepening the new US–Russia Cold War into an escape from it.[8]

The second vector is the residual portion of US policy toward Russia. The Obama administration insists that, central as the Ukrainian crisis is in shaping its policy, it has not displaced everything else. There remain areas where it seeks to cooperate with Moscow, and the role each played in reaching the Iranian nuclear deal makes the point. That is the problem. As a residual rather than a more equally weighted part of policy, it obstructs the ease with which the United States can integrate its short and long-term objectives. Finding ways to work with Russia in countering the Islamic State threat or manning the International Space Station should be approached not as useful remnants but as building blocks encouraging the search for other issues on which to cooperate. Doubtless the majority of these are in areas where the working groups under the Bilateral Presidential Commission were already at work. As many of these as possible should be resuscitated. Continuing to treat their suspension as the price Russia must pay for its actions in Ukraine, insisting that they be the victim of "no business as usual," holds hostage any attempt to advance an agenda that addresses the present without destroying the future.

The third vector is crucial; it constitutes the strategic dimension of policy. To the extent that the Obama administration's Russia policy has a strategic design, it is to isolate the Russian regime – though, as administration officials underscore, not the country itself. The sanctions, asset freezes, visa denials, abandoned negotiations, severed working contacts, suspended dialogue, and exclusion from Western clubs are all collectively designed to quarantine Putin and those on whom he bases his power and cast the regime as a pariah in the international community. Without question Russia has been successfully ostracized from any meaningful level of political and diplomatic intercourse with the West, but not isolated – not so long as other major powers, such as China, India, Brazil, and Turkey, along with a great portion of UN members, have not joined the US effort. Ostracism from the West is unquestionably a heavy price for Russia to pay. Whether, given Russia's other, admittedly inferior economic options, the price will be heavy enough to achieve US objectives remains to be demonstrated.

What needs no additional evidence, however, is that the United States has no hope of building a relationship with Russia that allows for anything close to the strategic vision urged here without engaging its leadership. As long as the basic thrust of US policy is to isolate Russia's government, and contact, when it occurs, is only about housekeeping, such as enforcing the Minsk ceasefire in eastern Ukraine or avoiding dangerous incidents between Russian ground forces and US aircraft in Syria, or confined to one-off instances of cooperation as against the Islamic State, important as that is, its larger purpose will be vague, inconstant, and tied to the evolution of current events.

It would be a fanciful soul who imagined Putin's Russia or the United States under Obama or his successor readily reconsidering the course they are on and, with their minds focused ten years down the road, making ending their new Cold War a priority. Nothing favors the long view. The anger and anxieties on both sides are too intense; the politics in both countries too unfavorable; and the cumulative damage from the past, including the layered mistrust, too great. But the confrontation in its current form will not last. That it could lead to something much worse cannot be ruled out. Neither side wants that, however, and, if the Ukrainian crisis can be managed, each is likely to begin softening its position - the United States not least because its European allies will gradually lose their stomach for maintaining the current sanctions regime. Indeed, by autumn 2015 both sides began to treat the soured relationship as "the new normal." Horizons were narrowing. The assumption - either explicit or at the back of people's mind - began to take hold in Moscow and Washington that the two had entered an indefinite era of uneasy rivalry, perhaps relieved by rare moments of limited cooperation. Then suddenly the attacks in Paris and the other near simultaneous acts of ISIL terrorism intruded, and the "new normal" seemed less frozen and barren.

As the new US–Russia Cold War enters this second phase, if that be the case, and in fitful fashion Moscow and Washington re-engage, the tendency will be to assume that US–Russian relations are returning to the familiar ups and downs of the past. But that will be a misapprehension. There is no going back. Whatever the commerce, the communication, the cooperation, at a deeper level the mistrust will remain. The same week that Putin instructed the Russian navy operating in the Mediterranean to coordinate with the French navy and spoke of an easing of tensions with the West, the Russian newspaper *Izvestiya* ran an article accusing the United States of destroying the social fabric of Russian society by financing Russia's LGBT community and adding to the country's demographic crisis by supplying medicines for cervical cancer that rendered women infertile(Grigorian, 2015). About the same time, Tom Cotton, a Republican senator from Arkansas, criticized "Obama's unwise decision to treat Russia as a legitimate partner in negotiations over Syria's future" and warned that, "right now, the United States is losing the proxy war in Syria - and a wider competition for regional influence - against Russia. And it will continue to do so without a dramatic shift in policy to confront Russian aggression" (Cotton, 2015).

The two countries, however, will have to deal with each other, because a wall like that between the United States and Iran or the United States and Cuba simply cannot be. But the two countries are now estranged, and that estrangement will not disappear even if they return to a more normal pattern of interaction - even if the IS threat drives them together. A Ukrainian crisis in stasis, rather than resolved, will keep in place many of the punitive measures imposed by the United States at the height of the crisis, a standing reminder that the United States sees Russia as a problem, not as a partner. The unexpected event will intervene, often the kind that fuels tension between the two countries, and neither will be particularly disposed to let differences slide. Nor in this new phase are leadership and publics in either country more likely than before to be moved by or even particularly focused on the larger stakes they have in the relationship.

Still, as the confrontation evolves, provided the worst is avoided, there will be opportunity for thoughtful reflection on both sides. To judge from a bold and wise essay by Andrei Kortunov (2015), the director general of the Russian International Affairs Council, that potential certainly exists in Russia, and he is scarcely alone. His constructive and acute analysis of the challenges facing his country, many of them fundamental but overlooked, is a plea for larger thinking. He points to the damaging impact on Russia's plans for Eurasia integration of worsening relations with the West; to an approaching "shortage of human resources" worse than any in Russia's "post-Soviet history"; to the defects in Russian soft power when soft power is more important than ever before; and to the need to nurture a Russian patriotism that "looks to the future not the past," one focused less on Russia as "a 'besieged fortress'" and more on building bonds around "hopes and ambitions" for the country. He is mindful that, during a crisis – and he sees Russia's relations with the West in crisis – "tactics dominate strategizing, and decision-making is largely determined by the rigid logic of the events taking place today, rather than the long-term consequences of the widening crisis spiral." But, as he reminds people, putting fundamental interests in perspective is crucial. If one of those is – as it surely must be – the modernization of the country, then he asks "have there been any successful projects of economic modernization carried out in isolation from the Euro-Atlantic core of the world economy?" That, Kortunov stresses, remains true even today of the BRICS, the countries Russia counts on for relief as economic ties with the West fray. As for the US–Russian relationship, he acknowledges how damaged it is, but argues that "the short term goal of confrontation management should not become a substitute for a longer-term goal of building a strategic partnership – a goal that becomes more compelling when leaders raise their eyes to the real security interests at stake.

One can hope that the longer a US–Russian Cold War persists, with its costs mounting and the larger challenges that it leaves unaddressed becoming more obvious, voices like Kortunov's will grow on both sides, gradually invading the consciousness of the political world and those responsible for securing their country's national security both today and for generations to come. The sooner that happens, the sooner making the new Cold War as short and shallow as possible stands a chance. The longer that takes, the more the wisdom of an earlier US president, Dwight Eisenhower, will apply: "Neither a wise man nor a brave man lies down on the tracks of history to wait for the train of the future to run over him."

Notes

Chapter 1 Dueling Concepts

1   I realize that, by this point in the book, there will be readers who believe that the focus on "the mess the two countries are in" simply misses the point. The problem for such readers is not what the two sides have done or are doing but, as anticipated in the introduction, Putin's aggression in Ukraine, actions that have torn up the previous political script and laid siege to security in Europe. Moreover, the source of the problem is to be found not in parsing the dynamics leading up to the Ukrainian crisis but in the nature of the Putin regime. In this mix the decisive factor is Russian behavior, and Russian behavior has been and will be driven overwhelmingly by the need to shore up the domestic political pillars of that regime. That I believe this oversimplifies a complex reality ought to be plain enough. Without denying the enormously destructive effect of Russia's seizure of Crimea and clandestine war in Donbas or the role that domestic factors play in Russian foreign policy generally, I think this fundamentally misreads what has brought the two countries to this point, and, in the process, it provides a poor guide for US policy. What lies ahead for the reader is my effort to piece together that more complex reality.

2   The expression "lands in between" has historically been applied to Poland, Hungary, and Czechoslovakia, whose fate, caught between Russia and Germany, had such a tragic effect on Europe's history in the nineteenth century and the interwar period in the twentieth century.

3   The literature is extensive. A representative sample can be found
    in the bibliography in Cameron G. Thies, A social psychological
    approach to enduring rivalries, *Political Psychology*, 22/4 (2001),
    pp. 722-5.

4   This is taken from the April 12, 1950, "Report to the National
    Security Council" (NSC 68), the famous NSC document setting
    out the fundamental objectives and direction for US foreign and
    defense policy. A copy of the original text can be found at https:
    //www.trumanlibrary.org/whistlestop/study_collections/coldwar/
    documents/pdf/10-1.pdf.

5   As already noted, a few US observers even lay the heaviest blame
    on their side. But so did a few during the original Cold War, such as
    Fleming (1961).

6   But Huntington did turn out to be very wrong on one point: "If civi-
    lization is what counts, however, the likelihood of violence between
    Ukrainians and Russians should be low. They are two Slavic, pri-
    marily Orthodox peoples who have had close relationships with
    each other for centuries."

Chapter 2 The Cold War

1   This reading of Putin's comment is almost as misleading as the
    misinterpretation of Nikita Khrushchev's famous remark "We will
    bury you." Khrushchev was not saying that the Soviet Union would
    crush the West. He was saying that the West was doomed by history
    and that the Soviet Union would be at its funeral. Similarly, Putin
    was not saying that this "catastrophe" must be reversed. He was
    underscoring the wreckage that it had left in Russia and how large
    the obstacles were on the path to political and economic reform.
    Both are good illustrations of the impact of statements taken out of
    context and turned into popular lore.

2   In September 1952, while ambassador in Moscow, Kennan drafted
    a 25-page memorandum in which, with remarkable prescience
    and subtlety, he corrected the general Western perception of Soviet

military intentions, described the counterproductive impact NATO had had, and provided a more refined notion of the actual nature of the threat the Soviet Union posed to the West. As he notes, it had absolutely no effect and, indeed, was scarcely read. This remarkable document is in his *Memoirs: 1950–1963* (1972, pp. 327–51).

3 This is from his article "Ленинская внешняя политика в современном мире" [Lenin's foreign policy in the modern world], *Communist*, no. 1 (January 1981), p. 1, cited in my essay "The 26th party congress and Soviet foreign policy," in Seweryn Bialer and Thane Gustafson (eds) *Russia at the Crossroads: The 26th Congress of the CPSU* (London: George Allen & Unwin, 1982), where I offer a far more complete analysis of the Soviet Union's thinking about détente.

4 Later that year, once the Soviet Union began to collapse, President Bush took the bold step of unilaterally reducing the large numbers of US sub-strategic weapons stored in Europe, and Moscow followed suit. But the chance to seize a Soviet initiative in order to eliminate them entirely was lost.

5 I heard him use the line in various forms on more than one occasion during these years.

6 This moment of decision-making late in the Bush administration is discussed in detail in Goldgeier and McFaul (2003, pp. 41–4).

Chapter 3 The Descent

1 The comment echoed a remark Obama had made on the eve of the June 2009 Moscow summit (Putin has "one foot in the old ways of doing business and one foot in the new"). Then his primary interlocutor was President Dmitri Medvedev, but he would pay a side visit to Putin, who was then prime minister. His elaboration this time, however, was far harsher.

2 Because, in the end game of US–Russian negotiations over the first round of NATO expansion, Yeltsin and his emissaries climbed down from their fiery but futile insistence that the decision be

reversed and seemed more concerned with minimizing the political damage to them back home – a concern the administration addressed with rewards, such as Russia's inclusion in the G-7 – many, including senior Clinton officials, persuaded themselves that Moscow had swallowed the NATO decision. They see subsequent Russian preoccupation with NATO moves as a subterfuge rather than a conviction. It is a view that survives today and colors the judgment of a good many, maybe most US and European observers in the current Ukrainian crisis.

3   He was not alone. I too, with a similar incautious bullishness, sketched the prospect of a US–Russian strategic partnership, in Robert Legvold, All the way: crafting a U.S.–Russian alliance, *National Interest*, 34/70 (2002-3), pp. 21-31.

4   The metaphor took on a life of its own as both the name for a US policy – like earlier the name "containment" – and a way of capturing a phase in US–Russian relations. For the Americans it was never meant to be more than a bridge from a low point in relations to something more stable and constructive. Drawn from computer talk second nature to the president and his senior Russia advisor, Michael McFaul (its author), it was not natural language for the Russian leadership. While they embraced the undertaking, it was, for the Russian side, a US initiative, and it remained so.

5   William J. Burns, The United States and Russia in a new era: one year after "reset," speech at the Center for American Progress, April 14, 2010. This idea was also stressed by Michael McFaul, in the Conference call briefing with administration officials on President Medvedev's visit to the White House on June 22, 2010 (www. whitehouse.gov/the-press-office/conference-call-briefing-with-ad ministration-officials-president-medvedevs-visit-wh).

6   The working group, part of the Euro-Atlantic Security Initiative, was co-chaired by Stephen Hadley, President Bush's national security advisor and long involved with the missile defense issue; Volker Rühe, the former German defense minister and an architect of NATO enlargement; and Vyacheslav Trubnikov, a former Russian deputy foreign minister and former head of the Foreign Intelligence Service. The group worked out the details of such a

system, the principles that should underlie it, and even its physical design (jointly sketched by General Trey Obering, the former head of the US Missile Defense Agency, and General Victor Esin, the last chief of staff of the Soviet Strategic Rocket Forces). Their report, entitled *The Game Changer: Cooperative Missile Defense*, can be found at http://carnegieendowment.org/globalten/?fa=50173.

7   It should not be – but probably is – necessary to underscore that an attempt to understand Russian actions is not the same as identifying with them. More simply put, getting Putin right does not mean one thinks he is right.

Chapter 4 Where To?

1   No one has discussed this trend more thoughtfully or completely than Alexei Arbatov in *An Unnoticed Crisis: The End of the History of Arms Control?* (Carnegie Moscow Center, June 2015).

2   These and the other many complex dimensions of developments in the Arctic are well explored in Lassi Heininen, Alexander Sergunin, and Gleb Yarovoy, *Russian Strategies in the Arctic: Avoiding a New Cold War* (Moscow: Valdai Discussion Club, September 2014). I have discussed in somewhat greater detail than here these new military trends in "A melting Arctic in a frozen Russia–West relationship," Valdai Discussion Club Online, June 5, 2015, http://valdaiclub.com/russia_and_the_world/77220.html.

3   To call for US–Russian–Chinese leadership in the nuclear sphere, it should be underscored, is not to assume the three will be able to jointly negotiate trilateral agreements binding all three countries in similar formats. As Alexey Arbatov has stressed to me, the asymmetries in capabilities between China and the other two are and will remain too great to permit that. But all three will have to take a lead in promoting understandings, norms, and bilateral agreements that form the webbing for a broader, more complex set of constraints appropriate to a world of nine nuclear powers.

4 To be more precise, rather than (as the EU did from 2003 when developing the four "common spaces") insist that Russia conform almost wholly to EU standards and ways of doing business, when Russia remained so fundamentally different, the objective might have been to find ways of reconciling – or at least, minimizing the differences between – the two contrasting models. This, of course, would also have required Russia to meet the EU halfway.

5 Hence, the undertaking would be unique and fundamentally different from more familiar past and present Track II dialogues. These are useful, but incapable of serving the purpose urged here.

6 It actually entailed a fairly elaborate effort on the US part, the details of which are in J. F. Matlock, *Reagan and Gorbachev: How the Cold War Ended* (New York: Random House, 200), ch. 3.

7 The Euro-Atlantic Security Initiative, as this trilateral initiative was called, was co-chaired by former Senator Sam Nunn, former Ambassador Wolfgang Ischinger, and former Foreign Minister Igor Ivanov. It included members who had served as foreign, defense, and prime ministers from across the Euro-Atlantic region, all of whom knew intimately the challenges in building such a community. Their final report and the reports of EASI's major working groups can be found at http://carnegieendowment.org/specialprojects/EuroAtlanticSecurityInitiativeEASI/.

8 An expert and very thoughtful analysis of what these might be can be found in Govan (2015).

References

Albright, M. K. 1998. Address to the U.S.-Russian Business Council, Chicago.

Arbatov, A. G. 2004. Military reform: from crisis to stagnation, in S. E. Miller and D. Trenin (eds) *The Russian Military: Power and Policy*. Cambridge, MA: MIT Press.

BBC 2015. Ukraine crisis: Kerry has "frank" meeting with Putin, May 12, www.bbc.com/news/world-europe-32700259.

Belfast Telegraph 2015. West "must rearm for new Cold War," *Belfast Telegraph*, January 8, www.belfasttelegraph.co.uk/news/northern-ireland/west-must-rearm-for-new-cold-war-30892319.html.

Biden, J. 2011. Vice President Joseph Biden, remarks at Moscow State University.

Biden, J. 2015a. Brookings hosts Vice President Joe Biden for remarks on the Russia–Ukraine Conflict, Brookings Institution.

Biden, J. 2015b. Remarks by the Vice President at the Munich Security Conference.

Braithwaite, R. 2015. Foreword, in D. Cadier and M. Light (eds) *Russia's Foreign Policy: Ideas, Domestic Politics, and External Relations*. Basingstoke: Palgrave Macmillan.

Brown, A. 2012. The Gorbachev revolution and the end of the Cold War, in M. P. Leffler and O. A. Westad (eds) *Cambridge History of the Cold War*, Vol. 3: *Endings*. Cambridge: Cambridge University Press.

Brzezinski, Z. 1972. How the Cold War was played, *Foreign Affairs*, 51(1).

Burns, W. J. 2009. Remarks at the Russia World Forum.

Clinton, H. 2011. America's pacific century, *Foreign Policy Online,* October 11, http://foreignpolicy.com/2011/10/11/americas-pacific-century/.

Clinton, W. J. 1993. Speech of the president to the American Society of Newspaper Editors, United States Naval Academy. Office of the Press Secretary, the White House.

Cotton, T. 2015. Proxy wars: Russia's intervention in Syria and what Washington should do, *Foreign Affairs,* Snapshot, November 24.

Davis, J. H. 2015. Task for Obama at Group of 7 is to reinforce isolation of Russia, *New York Times,* June 6.

EASI (Euro-Atlantic Security Initiative) 2012. *Toward a Euro-Atlantic Security Community.* Washington DC: Carnegie Endowment for International Peace.

EASI Working Group on Energy. 2012. *Energy as a Building Block in Creating a Euro-Atlantic Security Community.* Washington, DC: Carnegie Endowment for International Peace.

Edwards, J., and Kemp, J. 2006. *Russia's Wrong Direction: What the United States Can and Should Do.* New York: Council on Foreign Relations.

English, R. D. 2000. *Russia and the Idea of the West: Gorbachev, Intellectuals, and the End of the Cold War.* New York: Columbia University Press.

English, R. D. 2003. The road(s) not taken: causality and contingency in analysis of the Cold War, in W. C. Wohlforth (ed.) *Cold War Endgame: Oral History, Analysis, Debates.* University Park: Pennsylvania State University Press.

Fleming, D. F. 1961. *The Cold War and its Origins, 1917–1960.* Garden City, NY: Doubleday.

Frear, T., Kearns, I., and Kulesa, Ł. 2015. *Preparing for the Worst: Are Russian and NATO Military Exercises Making War in Europe More Likely?* European Leadership Network Policy Brief, www.europeanleadershipnetwork.org/medialibrary/2015/08/07/ea2b8c22/Preparing%20for%20the%20Worst.pdf.

Fukuyama, F. 1992. *The End of History and the Last Man.* New York: Free Press.

Gaddis, J. L. 1997. *We Now Know: Rethinking Cold War History.* Oxford: Clarendon Press.

Gaddis, J. L. 2005. *The Cold War: A New History*. New York: Peguin Press.

Garthoff, R. L. 1994. *The Great Transition: American–Soviet Relations and the End of the Cold War*. Washington, DC: Brookings Institution.

Garthoff, R. L. 2015. *Soviet Leaders and Intelligence: Assessing the American Adversary during the Cold War*. Washington, DC: Georgetown University Press.

Ghemawat, P., and Altman, S. A. 2015. *DHL Global Connectedness Index 2014*. New York: NYU Stern School of Business and IESE Business School.

Goldgeier, J. M., and McFaul, M. 2003. *Power and Purpose: U.S. Policy toward Russia after the Cold War*. Washington, DC: Brookings Institution.

Govan, G. G. 2015. Conventional arms control in Europe: some thoughts about an uncertain future, *Deep Cuts Issue Brief #5*, http://deepcuts.org/files/pdf/Deep_Cuts_Issue_Brief5_Conventional_Arms_Control_in_Europe(1).pdf.

Graham, T. E. 2012. Где искать будущее [Where to look for the future], *Ekspert*, November 16, http://expert.ru/expert/2012/46/gde-iskat-buduschee/?n=87778.

Grigorian, A., and Zmanovskaya, A. 2015. США разочаровались в российской оппозиции и ставят на ЛГБТ-движения [US betting on LGBT movement, not disappointed in it], Известия [Izvestia], November 17.

Halliday, F. 1999. *Revolution and World Politics: The Rise and Fall of the Sixth Great Power*. London: Macmillan.

Haslam, J. 2011. *Russia's Cold War: From the October Revolution to the Fall of the Wall*. New Haven, CT: Yale University Press.

Hill, F., and Pifer, S. 2015. Putin's risky game of chicken, *New York Times*, June 15, www.nytimes.com/2015/06/16/opinion/putins-risky-game-of-chicken.html?_r=0.

Hughes, P. M. 1997. A DIA global security assessment, *DISAM Journal*, summer, pp. 88–98; www.disam.dsca.mil/pubs/Vol%2019_4/Hughes.pdf.

Huntington, S. P. 1993. The clash of civilizations?, *Foreign Affairs*, 72(3), pp. 22–49.

Ikenberry, G. J. 2014. The illusion of geopolitics: the enduring power of the liberal order, *Foreign Affairs*, 93(3), pp. 80–91.

Ivanov, I. S. 2014. From Munich to Sochi, November 6, http://russian council.ru/en/inner/?id_4=4734#top.

Ivanov, I. S. 2015. The sunset of Greater Europe, September 12, http://russiancouncil.ru/en/inner/?id_4=6564#top-content.

Jervis, R. 2001. Was the Cold War a security dilemma?, *Journal of Cold War Studies*, 3(1), pp. 36–60.

Karaganov, S. 2014a. Western delusions triggered conflict and Russians will not yield, *Financial Times*, September 14.

Karaganov, S. 2014b. Долгая конфронтация (A long confrontation), *Izvestiya*, September 3.

Kennan, G. 1947. The sources of Soviet conduct, *Foreign Affairs*, 25(4), pp. 566–82.

Kennan, G. F. 1972. *Memoirs, 1925–1950*. Boston: Little, Brown.

Kennan, G. F. 1997. A fateful error, *New York Times*, February 5.

Kennedy, J. F. 1963. Commencement address at American University, June 10.

Kissinger, H. A. 1972. Congressional briefing, Washington, DC: White House.

Kortunov, A. 2015. A new agenda for Russian foreign policy, in *The U.S. Response to Russia's Assertiveness: Economic, Military and Diplomatic Challenges*. Washington, DC: Aspen Institute Congressional Program; www.aspeninstitute.org/sites/default/files/content/up load/2015-Russia.Conference.Report.Berlin.pdf.

Krauthammer, C. 1994. The romance with Russia is over, *Washington Post*, December 16.

Kremenyuk, V. A. 2015. *Уроки холодной войны* [Lessons of the Cold War]. Moscow: Aspect Press.

Kristensen, H. M. 2014. W 80-1 warhead selected for new nuclear cruise missile, *Federation of American Scientists*, https://fas.org/blogs/security/2014/10/w80-1_lrso/.

Kurlantzick, J. 2015. The great deglobalizing, *Boston Globe*, February 1.

Lamothe, D. 2015. Russia is greatest threat to the U.S., says Joint Chiefs chairman nominee Gen. Joseph Dunford, *Washington Post*, July 9, https://www.washingtonpost.com/news/checkpoint/

wp/2015/07/09/russia-is-greatest-threat-to-the-u-s-says-joint-chi efs-chairman-nominee-gen-joseph-dunford/.

Lavrov, S. 2014. Remarks by Foreign Minister Sergey Lavrov at the XXII Assembly of the Council on Foreign and Defence Policy, Moscow, 22 November.

Leffler, M. P., and Westad, O. A. 2010. *The Cambridge History of the Cold War*, vols 1–3. Cambridge: Cambridge University Press.

Lippmann, W. 1947. *The Cold War: A Study in US Foreign Policy since 1945*. New York: Harper.

Lucas, E. 2007. *The New Cold War: How the Kremlin Menaces Both Russia and the West*. London: Bloomsbury.

Mandelbaum, M. 2002. *The Ideas that Conquered the World*. New York: Public Affairs.

Matlock, J. F. 2004. *Reagan and Gorbachev: How the Cold War Ended*. New York: Random House.

Matlock, J. 2015. 2015 EPIIC Symposium: Russia in the 21st Century, ASEAN Auditorium, Tufts University, February 27; https://www.youtube.com/watch?v=A-J0hZ9HpWo.

MacKinnon, M. 2007. *The New Cold War: Revolutions, Rigged Elections and Pipeline Politics in the Former Soviet Union*. London, Carroll & Graf.

Mead, W. R. 2014. The return of geopolitics: the revenge of the revisionist powers, *Foreign Affairs*, 93(3), pp. 69–79.

Mearsheimer, J. 2014. Why the Ukraine crisis is the West's fault: the liberal delusions that provoked Putin, *Foreign Affairs*, 93(5), pp. 77–89.

Mecklin, J. 2015. Disarm and modernize, *Foreign Policy Online*, https://foreignpolicy.com/2015/03/24/disarm-and-modernize-nuclear-weapons-warheads/.

Medvedev, D. 2010. Speech by Dmitry Medvedev, president of the Russian Federation, at the meeting with Russian ambassadors and permanent representatives to international organizations, Russian Foreign Ministry.

NATO 1991. The alliance's new strategic concept agreed by the heads of state and government participating in the meeting of the North Atlantic Council, www.nato.int/cps/en/natohq/official_texts_23847.htm.

Obama, B. 2009. Remarks of the president at the New Economic School graduation, Moscow, July 7, https://www.whitehouse.gov/the-press-office/remarks-president-new-economic-school-graduation.

Obama, B. 2014. Statement by the President on Ukraine, March 20, https://www.whitehouse.gov/the-press-office/2014/03/20/statement-president-ukraine.

Obama, B. 2015. Full transcript of BuzzFeed News' interview with President Barack Obama, February 11, www.buzzfeed.com/buzzfeednews/full-transcript-of-buzzfeed-news-interview-with-president#.tdqPX1jjX.

Orwell, G. 1945. You and the atomic bomb, *Tribune*, October 19.

OSCE 2010. Astana commemorative declaration: towards a security community, December 3, www.osce.org/node/74985.

Patrushev, N. 2014. Вторая "холодная" [The second "cold"], *Rossiiskaya gazeta*, October 15, www.rg.ru/2014/10/15/patrushev.html.

Pickering, T. 2015. Thomas Pickering on diplomacy, Iran, Korea, Russia, realpolitik, and the ethics of war, *Bulletin of the Atomic Scientists*, June 30.

Pravda, A. 2014. Don't call it a new Cold War: partnership with Russia is not damaged beyond repair, *European Leadership Network*, October 24, www.europeanleadershipnetwork.org/dont-call-it-a-new-cold-war-partnership-with-russia-is-not-damaged-beyond-repair-_2048.html?utm_source=ELN+Newsletter&utm_campaign=6ebeac9f83-Systemic+Imbalance&utm_medium=email&utm_term=0_8e6b30e571-6ebeac9f83-&mc_cid=6ebeac9f83&mc_eid=%5bUNIQID%5d&utm_source=ELN+Newsletter&utm_campaign=6ebeac9f83Negotiating+with+Moscow&utm_medium=email&utmterm=0_8e6b30e571-6ebeac9f83-100242497&mc_cid=6ebeac9f83&mc_eid=eae437a398.

Putin, V. 2001. Speech by RF President V.V. Putin in response to questions by journalists at the joint press conference with U.S. President George Bush, November 13, www.nuclearfiles.org/menu/

key-issues/nuclear-weapons/issues/arms-control-disarmament/
us_russia_treaties/moscow_treaty/putin_speech_in_response_to_
journalist_questions_at_joint_press_conference.pdf.

Putin, V. 2005. Послание Федеральному Собранию Российской Федерации [Address to the Federal Assembly of the Russian Federation].

Putin, V. 2007. Speech and the following discussion at the Munich Conference on Security Policy.

Putin, V. 2014a. Address by the president of the Russian Federation, St George's Hall, Kremlin Palace.

Putin, V. 2014b. Meeting of the Valdai International Discussion Club, Sochi.

Putin, V. 2015. Поздравление Президенту США Бараку Обаме с национальным праздником – Днём независимости [Congratulations on the occasion of President Barack Obama's national holiday – Independence Day], July 4, www.kremlin.ru/events/president/news/49864.

Rehman, I. 2015. *Murky Waters: Naval Nuclear Dynamics in the Indian Ocean*. Washington, DC: Carnegie Endowment for International Peace.

Remnick, D. 1992. The trial of the old regime, *New Yorker*. November 30, p. 104.

Rice, C. 2000. Campaign 2000: promoting the national interest, *Foreign Affairs*, 79(1), pp. 45–62.

Rojansky, M. 2015. The geopolitics of European security and cooperation: the consequences of US–Russia tension, in *The U.S. Response to Russia's Assertiveness: Economic, Military and Diplomatic Challenges*. Washington, DC: Aspen Institute Congressional Program; www.aspeninstitute.org/sites/default/files/content/upload/2015-Russia.Conference.Report.Berlin.pdf.

Rozman, G. 2014. *The Sino-Russian Challenge to the World Order*. Washington, DC: Woodrow Wilson Center Press.

Sanger, D. E. 2001. The Bush–Putin summit, *New York Times*, November 16, www.nytimes.com/2001/11/16/world/bush-putin-summit-ranch-before-after-bush-putin-s-banter-no-agreement-missile.html.

Sankaran, J. 2015. Pakistan's battlefield nuclear policy: a risky solution to an exaggerated threat, *International Security*, 39(3), pp. 118–51.

Saull, R. 2011. Social conflict and the global Cold War, *International Affairs*, 87(5), pp. 1123–40.

Service, R. 2015. *The End of the Cold War: 1985–1991*. New York: Public Affairs.

Solozobov, Y. 2014. Контрполярный мир [Contrapolar world], *Izvestia*, December 9, http://izvestia.ru/news/580537#comments#ixzz3LTa Cz76C.

Stalin, J. 1950. Telegram from Stalin to Shtykov, January 30, History and Public Policy Program Digital Archive, AVP RF, Fond 059a, Opis 5a, Delo 3, Papka 11, list 92, http://digitalarchive.wilsoncenter.org/document/112136.

Stalin, J. 1952. *Economic Problems of Socialism in the USSR*. Moscow: International Publishers.

Stent, A. 2015. Forty years on: what can we learn from the Helsinki Final Act?, *Valdai Discussion Club*, August 5, http://valdaiclub.com/europe/80060.html.

Talbott, S. 2002. *The Russia Hand: A Memoir of Presidential Diplomacy*. New York: Random House.

Talbott, S. 2014. The making of Vladimir Putin, *Politico*, August 19, www.politico.com/magazine/story/2014/08/putin-the-backstory-110151.html#.VPYXFvAo4pJ.

Trenin, D. 2014a. *The Ukrainian Crisis and the Resumption of Great-Power Rivalry*, Carnegie Endowment for International Peace, http://carnegie.ru/2014/07/09/ukraine-crisis-and-resumption-of-great-power-rivalry/hfgs#.

Trenin, D. 2014b. Welcome to Cold War II: this is what it will look like, *Foreign Policy Online*, March 4, http://foreignpolicy.com/2014/03/04/welcome-to-cold-war-ii/.

Trenin, D. 2014c. West and Russia now in permanent crisis, *Global Times*, November 4, http://carnegie.ru/publications/?fa=57156.

Trilateral Commission 2014. A North American perspective, in P. Dobriansky, A. Olechowski, Y. Satoh, and I. Yurgens (eds) *Engaging Russia: A Return to Containment?* Washington, DC: Trilateral Commission.

Ulam, A. B. 1974. *Expansion and Coexistence: Soviet Foreign Policy 1917–1973*. New York: Praeger.

US Department of Defense 2015. *National Military Strategy*. Washington, DC: US GPO.

Varandani, S. 2015. Putin puts Russia's Northern Fleet on full combat alert in the Arctic amid security concerns, *International Business Times*, March 16, www.ibtimes.com/putin-puts-russias-northern-fleet-full-combat-alert-arctic-amid-security-concerns-1848008.

Voigt, K. 2014. A new phase of Russia and Ostpolitik has begun, October 23, American Institute for Contemporary German Studies, www.aicgs.org/issue/a-new-phase-of-russia-and-ostpolitik-has-begun/.

Walt, S. M. 2014. The bad old days are back, *Foreign Policy Online*, May 2, http://foreignpolicy.com/2014/05/02/the-bad-old-days-are-back/?utm_source=Sailthru&utm_medium=email&utm_term=Flashpoints&utm_campaign=2014_FlashPoints%20RS%20bestofonline2014.

Weinberger, C. W., and Schweizer, P. 1997. Russia's oil grab, *New York Times*, May 9, www.nytimes.com/1997/05/09/opinion/russia-s-oil-grab.html.

Weisgerber, M. 2015. Pentagon moves money to counter Russia, *Defense One*, July 8, www.defenseone.com/threats/2015/07/pentagon-moves-money-counter-russia/117319/.

Westad, O. A. 2007. *The Global Cold War: Third World Interventions and the Making of our Times*. Cambridge: Cambridge Univesity Press.

Westad, O. A. 2013. *Reviewing the Cold War: Approaches, Interpretations, Theory*. London: Routledge.

White House Office of the Press Secretary. 1992. A charter for American–Russian partnership and friendship, June 17, http://fas.org/spp/starwars/offdocs/b920617b.htm.

Will, G. 2014. Top US journalists agree: "Putin is like Hitler." Worse than ISIS, worse than Stalin, *Russia Insider*, November 1, http://russia-insider.com/en/tv_politics/2014/11/02/10-27-07am/top_us_journalists_agree_putin_hitler_worse_isis_worse_stalin.

Wilson, S. 2014. Obama dismisses Russia as "regional power" acting out of weakness, *Washington Post*, March 25.

Wines, M. 1992. Bush and Yeltsin declare formal end to Cold War: agree to exchange visits, *New York Times*, February 2.

Wohlforth, W. C. (ed.) 2003. *Cold War Endgame: Oral History, Analysis, Debates*. University Park: Pennsylvania State University Press.

Zamyatin, T. 2015. BRICS, SCO look sound alternatives to Russia's strategic partnership with West – experts, *TASS*, June 10.

Zhdanov, A. 1947. Report on the international situation to the Cominform, Szklarska Poręba, Poland, September 22, http://ciml.250x.com/archive/cominform_index.html.

Zubok, V. M. 2003. Gorbachev and the end of the Cold War: different perspectives on the historical personality, in W. C. Wohlforth (ed.) *Cold War Endgame: Oral History, Analysis, Debates*. University Park: Pennsylvania State University Press.

Zubok, V. M. and Pleshakov, C. 1996. *Inside the Kremlin's Cold War: from Stalin to Khrushchev*. Cambridge, MA: Harvard University Press.

Index